VALENTINE TREASURY

A Century of Valentine Cards

Robert Brenner

77 Lower Valley Road, Atglen, PA 19310

Dedication

It is to anyone
who has sent or received a valentine
that I dedicate this book.
May the memories of that valentine greeting remain with you.
While life is indeed short, the greetings we send
and the good deeds we accomplish
will live long after our physical presence.
May anyone who has not yet sent a valentine,
be inspired to do so
after reading the pages that follow.
Love has created for all of us
some wonderful examples of artistic craftsmanship
in loving valentine cards.

Library of Congress Cataloging-in-Publication Data

Brenner, Robert.
    Valentines / Robert Brenner.
        p. cm.
    Includes index.
    ISBN 0-7643-0195-0 (hardcover)
    1. Valentines--Collectors and collecting--Catalogs. I. Title.
NC 1866.V3B74 1997
741.6'84--dc20   96-36140
                                    CIP

Copyright © 1997 by Robert Brenner

Designed by Joy Shih Ng
Printed in China
ISBN: 0-7643-0195-0

Published by Schiffer Publishing Ltd.
77 Lower Valley Road
Atglen, PA 19310
Telephone: 610-593-1777
Fax: 610-593-2002
Please write for a free catalog.
This book may be purchased from the publisher.
Please include $2.95 for shipping.
Try your bookstore first.

We are interested in hearing from authors
with book ideas on related subjects.

CONTENTS

Acknowledgments

Without the generous understanding, motivation, and help of many individuals this book would have never been possible. I especially wish to thank Doug Congdon-Martin for his editorial skills, but most of all for his photography expertise. Hours of careful handling and delicate maneuvering were necessary to photograph the hundreds of valentines contained herein. Doug's patience and kind suggestions help complete this book in a way which would have never been possible without his input. Extra thanks go to Joy Ng who provided the artistic skills to create a book of this magnitude. I sincerely appreciate the countless hours that she put forth to create this work.

Special thanks go to my wife Sharon who spent many hours helping with various aspects of this book as well as picking up household duties when I was writing. It is Sharon's collection that illustrates the vast, colorful, and creative range of valentine history contained in this book. Her editorial skills and suggestions were of tremendous help in this project.

Once again a project of this magnitude would be impossible without qualified and smiling librarians. Even though Princeton is rural and somewhat isolated geographically, our Internet connection to the entire world and a library staff dedicated to searching diligently for answers to some very difficult requests are truly blessings. Thanks go to Lorraine Cederholm, our head librarian who spends numerous hours helping everyone who asks for her assistance. Princeton's head librarian is far above her league in intelligence, dedication, and professional skills. Thanks also go to other staff and volunteers who helped to complete this book: Shirley Hamaishi, Tammy Kiefer, Ruby Keller, and Marge Philbrick.

Thanks go to the following friends and associates who provided so much help in many different ways: Evalene Pulati, Jim and Roberta Fiene, Don Rintz, Laura and Craig Beane, Beatrice Blumchen, Jerry Ehernberger, Mike Makurat, Jeffrey Swanson, Fred Studach, Lorraine Otto, Karen Brown, Susan Brown Nicholson, and all who have touched our lives.

Finally, I wish to thank all those who have created these magnificent works of art sent on Valentine's Day for so many years. Without this artistic creativity and dedicated craftsmanship, such examples of cards would never have been possible. But most of all, we need to thank the people who saved their cards so that our generation might appreciate their beauty.

Chapter I
Beginnings of Valentine Traditions

Origins and early customs of St. Valentine's Day

Shakespeare and Chaucer allude to St. Valentine's Day, of course, and so did John Dryden whose often overlooked poems speak of this holiday. One of his most exquisite poems, "To His Valentine," documents the writing of love verses to a favorite lover on this holiday. For centuries great writers have spoken of this holiday and its significance in our culture. Its roots and early customs are intriguing to document.

Religion combined with superstition formed most of the early observance customs of this day. Valentine's Day was observed in England as early as 1446. Chaucer wrote that it was the day the birds paired off. Many young, single women believed it was much more consequential to their pairing off. In Derbyshire, England, they circled the church twelve times at midnight repeating, "I sow hempseed, hempseed I sow, he that loves me best, come after me now." At the completion of the twelfth round of the church without stopping, it was believed that the lover would appear and follow.

Some hopefuls pinned five bay leaves to their pillows on Valentine's eve. One leaf pinned to the center and one to each corner invoked dreams of their future husbands. In some places an unmarried girl would strike her forehead with a folded rose petal. If the petal cracked, she was assured of her Valentine's true love. Marriage obviously ended the practice of these customs. For the new bride the guessing, the waiting, the insecurity was over.

Other customs were practiced, one of which was the baking of a "Dumb" cake, so termed because it was mixed and baked without speaking. After being taken out of the oven, the cook ascended the stairs backwards and placed the cake under her pillow. This custom would insure her dreaming that evening of her lover. Another was the writing of the lover's name on a piece of paper at midnight, burning it, and laying the ashes wrapped in paper on a looking glass, which had been marked previously with a cross. All of this was placed under the young woman's pillow and dreams of her lover would result as well from this practice. Still another interesting English custom included finding a closed door on Valentine's Day and throwing in a valentine attached to an apple or orange. The door was then rapped loudly, and the messenger hurried away.

Another custom which lead to many carefully laid plans, and sometimes to cunning stratagem, was based on the superstition that the first person encountered on Valentine morning was either a destined husband or wife, or at least a valentine for the year. Many a door was not opened on that morning until the right person should appear.

In some districts of Norfolk, England, the children set out to "catch" valentines, the implication being, that if a youngster could say to an adult twice "Good morrow Valentine," before the youngster was spoken to, and before the sun had risen, a present was the reward. If the sun had risen, the present could be held back, on the grounds that the young child was "sunburnt."

Two of the more popular rhymes to evolve from this custom are recorded:

> Good morrow to you, Valentine;
> Curl your locks as I do mine,
>
> Two before and three behind
> Good morrow to you, Valentine.
>
> Good morrow, Valentine;
> First 'tis yours, then 'tis mine;
> So please give me a Valentine.

Thus the first of many verses orally given by youngsters to gain a present or reward was documented in Hertfordshire, in the early 1600s. John Donne, too, is worth browsing into for early Valentine verse, as in his Epitalamium on the marriage of the Princess Elizabeth to Frederick Count Valentine,

St. Valentine's Day, 1614. Perhaps the earliest writer of valentine verse of whom we have a record is Charles, Duke of Orleans, who was taken prisoner by the English at the Battle of Agincourt.

Thus St. Valentine's Day's early establishment as a holiday with deep sentiments and emotions is well documented. However, its early history and origins are more abstract as historians cannot completely agree on its start.

St. Valentine—Origins and early History

Who is Saint Valentine? Although the name of St. Valentine appears on calendars, the Church does little to observe him. In fact, only America and England keep his memory alive to any extent. Every year we send cards and observe this holiday. Each year museums dedicate exhibit space to old valentines which never fails to arouse nostalgic memories of the past. So it only seems appropriate to explore the life of this individual who has had such an effect on so many people on February 14 each year. Some say he was a Roman priest; others say he was the Bishop of Terni, a small town north of Rome. History cannot agree on which individual is the true name's sake for this day.

Tradition recounts that a Roman priest, Valeninus, was imprisoned for giving aid and comfort to the Christians during the pagan rule of Emperor Claudius II. History tells us that Claudius issued a decree forbidding Romans to marry (married men did not make the best soldiers), which Valeninus ignored. Instead, he encouraged young lovers to wed secretly with the blessings of the underground Christian church. When Claudius discovered these undercover marriages, he threw Valeninus in prison to be executed.

While in prison, Valeninus developed a friendship with his jailer's blind daughter and miraculously restored her sight. On the eve of his execution, Valeninus penned her a note, expressing his affection, and signed it "from your Valentine." Beheaded on February 14 sometime between 270 to 273 AD, he quickly became the favorite of lovers, and folklore quickly relayed the story of his life from village to village.

Others side with the story of the Bishop of Terni, a small town north of Rome. Reputedly this bishop was beheaded for converting a Roman family to Christianity in 273 A.D., thus incurring the wrath of the Romans.

Part of this confusion can be cleared up by exploring a few geographical and historical facts. Both were martyred at about the same time. Since history does accurately record St. Valentine as being born in Terni, which at that time was about 100 miles from Rome where he was reputed to have been beheaded, he might have been labeled a Roman bishop. The Bishop of Terni is venerated at Terni, where, within a small Basilica to his memory, is an altar containing his relics. In the small ancient church of St. Praxedes in Rome is a glass-fronted wooden box which contains some of the bones of St. Valentine, together with those of St. Zenone. It seems very plausible that the Bishop of Terni and the Roman priest are one and the same. His martyrdom, some historians say, was the origin of this holiday.

Some historians feel that its origins do not evolve from a single person, but from a pagan feast celebrated in Roman times. Lupercalia is an ancient Roman pagan feast that caused Valentine's Day to be associated with lovers. It fell annually in mid-February, February 15th, to be exact, and was celebrated to ensure fertility of people, flocks, and fields.

Young Roman men first would put the names of young girls into a box and then each would draw a name. The girl whose name is chosen by a young man would become his partner at the coming festival of Lupercalia. This day was changed to February 14 by Pope Gelasius in 496 to coincide with the date of the execution of Valenisus, therefore de-paganizing Lupercalia by changing both the name and the date.

These same historians feel that the popular belief as early as the fourteenth century that the birds begin to pair on this day eventually developed into the custom of young men and women choosing each other for Valentines on February 14 and then sending each other letters. It is this tradition that most doubtedly led to the popular custom of sending Valentine cards as we do today.

Late 1880s fold-out card employing intricate layers of blue flowers. $50-60.

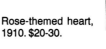

Rose-themed heart, 1910. $20-30.

Chapter II
Early Beginnings of Card Traditions: 1600-1799

Just where lies history's first reference to the tradition of sending cards? Perhaps our very first reference is to be found in a fourteenth century poem by John Lydgarte, in praise of Catherine, wife of Henry V.

> "Seynte Valentine of custome yeere by yeere
> Men have an usance, in this regioun
> To loke and serche Cupides kalendar,
> And chose theyr choyse by grete affeccioun,
> Such has been move with Cupides nocioun,
> Takying theyre choyse as theyre sort doth falle;
> but I love oon whiche excelleth alle."

Even before the traditional exchange of cards as we know it today, gift giving customs were firmly established. Valentine's Day traditions first included the exchange of presents on February 14. Those who could afford it gave gifts of precious jewels to their loves. This bestowal of gifts was introduced in the sixteenth and seventeenth centuries, primarily as an obligation on the part of men only, but later becoming a mutual responsibility. In addition to jewels, the sender would usually include an article of clothing accessory such as rings, bracelets, handkerchiefs, scarves, or a simple strip of blue ribbon with just a few lines of sentiment engagingly called posies. Nick, a farmer's son, when sending a yard of blue ribbon to Joan Hobson wrote:

> I sent you here of ribbon a whole yard;
> And money goeth with me very hard;
> For else this year two yards should be,
> Since I do hold nothing too dear for thee.

The custom of bestowing gifts reached its zenith in Norwich, England, when weeks beforehand, the city was in a state of mysterious preparation "with the streets swarmed with carriers and baskets laden with treasures" to be delivered on the different doorsteps. The messenger gave a loud knock, the louder the better, and, then hurried away into hiding, from where he could watch the present being taken indoors. This was a result of the custom which dictated that presents be given anonymously, or bearing only such messages as "Good morrow, Valentine."

While valentines have been sent since the early church fathers turned the Lupercalia into a Christian festival, the earliest documented valentine is 1667. Samuel Pepys, the celebrated chronicler of domestic life in England in the reign of Charles II, recorded in his diary numerous mentions of Valentine customs. One of the most significant entries, recorded in 1667, is another very early mention of such a card.

"This morning came up to my wife's bedside, (I being up dressing myself), little Will Mercer to be her Valentine; and brought her name writ upon blue paper in gold letters done by himself very pretty; and we both were very pleased with it. But I am also this year my wife's Valentine; and it will cost me. . .5; but that I must have laid out if we had not been Valentines." A little bit later Pepys added "I find that Mrs. Pierce's little girl is my Valentine, she having drawn me; which I was not sorry for, it easing me of something more than I must have given to others. But here I do observe fashion of drawing mottoes as well as names, so that Pierce who drew my wife, did draw also a motto, and this girl drew another for me. What mine was I forget but my wife's was 'Most courteous and most fair,' which, as it may be used on an anagram upon each name, might be very pretty. "

However, found in the Massachusetts Historical Society is a letter from John Cotton, a clergyman, who, in 1625, says that one of his young ministers came to him to say that two young girls in his parish wanted to draw for Valentine's, should he let them? "I told him," says Cotton, "that there might be no harm in it; but as the Bible was against witchcraft and things of chance, they better not draw."

The beginning of the eighteenth century saw paper Valentines established as a convenient and convincing symbol of affection. This century witnessed the beginning of the decorated valentine, which became more and more elaborate as time went on. How it all began is a mystery, but it is possible to believe that some swain decorated the margin of his verse with drawings, and that his lady love, on receiving it, showed the card to her girlfriends with pride and joy. They, in turn, bitten by jealous pangs, perhaps berated their own lovers into creating such sentiments. In any event, in this early time period all valentines were hand-made. Some were merely penned messages with a decorative border sketched in the same ink. Others were cutouts with pin-pricked designs or handcolored symbols, or both. Traditionally these early valentines were folded down to a small square with penned messages on each fold, together with a heart or floral motif.

When lithographed in black and white, they were hand-colored, and verses were penned at the bottom of the design. Water colors were applied by women primarily one by one and then valentines were sold to gentlemen for their lovers. These are among the rarest of valentines found today since very few were saved.

Early in the eighteenth century, around 1710, tiny valentines were produced, exquisitely cut by hand to resemble lace, and water-colored with love birds, hearts, pierced by arrows, and flowers. Oral history records that these valentines were created by nuns in Strasbourg who sold them to raise funds with which to carry on their charitable deeds. When artists such as Francesco Bartolozzi, one of the century's greatest stipple engravers, started making valentines, a business was quickly born. While most of these early valentines were manufactured in England, some were created in France.

A letter in 1745 found in the Massachussets Historical Society in Boston from a young girl, says, "Last Wednesday was St. Valentine's Day and Betty said I might dream of my sweetheart the night before. To make it double certain, I did gather five bay leaves. Four, I pinned to the corners of my pillow, and the fifth to the middle. To make it more certain, I did boil an egg, hard. I took out the yolk and filled the center with salt. Then I did eat it, shell and all, without drinking or speaking."

Thus the very beginnings of card sending were somewhat established as individuals sought to commemorate St. Valentine's Day in some fashion, be it a card, token, or oral greeting on that occasion.

Black and white lithograph, hand-colored and hand-written verse. $175-200.

Chapter III
Beginnings of the Golden Age:
1800-1849

Numerous historical references have been found in recent years which well document Valentine's Day customs in the 1800s. It was during this time that valentines began to take on more significance as the holiday gained popularity. One popular custom of this time was to tear a valentine in half, send one half to the chosen one with a message "Guess Who," retain the other half, and the following day, little groups met and matched halves. Of course, there was some disappointment and much joy depending upon the outcome. Another custom was for the young man to steal up to the door of his sweetheart, ring the doorbell or knocker, then run off to the shelter of a tree and wait for her to come to the door to claim her prize. He then would race home under the friendly darkness, his heart no doubt pounding with happiness.

But one of the most popular customs was the valentine box at school with the teacher playing cupid. When the pupils arrived at school on St. Valentine's Day, each deposited his treasure throve, hoping there were a few in the box for them. When the magic hour arrived, the teacher uncovered the box, gathered its contents, and one by one called out the names amidst a flutter of hearts. The teacher was always the luckiest as everyone in the class put a valentine in the box for the teacher, hoping that their teacher would remember this kindness in the months ahead. If a female teacher were lucky, she would have received a valentine box from one of her favorite pupils. These were very elaborate and costly items. Beautiful ribbons, flowers, feathers, and other adornments were assembled on the outside of the box. These boxes, primarily meant to hold cards, were also often decorated with chromos of angel and cherub. If a male teacher were lucky, he could receive a less decorated, more masculine box or some other token of appreciation befitting of a male.

Greetings Become Commercialized in Industrial Age

Previous to 1800, the only methods of graphic reproduction were woodcuts and steel engravings, both of which were extremely costly. However, that was to change in 1798 when Aloys Senefelder, an actor and playwright, found through a series of experiments that if he drew on finely grained limestone with a grease crayon, the crayoned sections would attract ink and repel water, whereas the empty parts would attract water and repel ink. Thus the infancy stages of lithography were created. Within the next decade, color was added to the process and chromolithography was born.

Each color required a separate stone and could be printed on top of one another. Additional colors had to be perfectly lined up on the paper with the original, or the entire print would be blurred. Somewhere between 1820 and 1825, steel embossing dies were invented, and embossing firms sprang up across Germany, the birthplace of chromolithography.

Most of these chromolithographers were located in Breslau, Poland, once part of Eastern Germany. The Englemann family established a firm there in 1815 with the Schwerpwaker Company and Mai Sohne also establishing themselves around 1820. In 1827, Adam Mamelok established Mamelok Press. Thus beautiful color scraps could now be quickly and economically produced. It was this process which speeded along the production of valentines as now beautiful chromolithographs and other commercially printed material could be easily added to valentines.

Valentines as paper love tokens appeared in the latter part of the eighteenth century. They were sheets of music with a colored picture at the top. Others were handmade by folding paper and cutting it with a pair of scissors or sharp knife into a very intricate and lacy design which was later colored. In the early part of this century color engraving, lithography, and aquatint were the processes used in their making. The "Endless Knot of Love" was one of the popular forms at this time. The message was intertwined in the form of a maze and the whole design was left uncolored or colored by hand.

Historical figures made numerous references to the custom of Valentine verses and cards in the early 1800s. "Amid these wilds I wonder in despair, I sigh for her so faithless yet so fair, Ye streams, Ye words, Ye breezes tell the agony of soul for her I feel." Such is a verse from an "Unrequited Valentine," in Lord Byron's memory. Byron, a well-known English poet, was a real rogue who had many love affairs. Dying in 1824 at the age of 36, his uncle Richard E. Byron, a famous English etcher, supposedly created these valentines in memory of his nephew. The first issue of this series was by the firm of Addenbrooke, an early English manufacturer of valentines, in 1828.

The earliest manufacturer of embossed valentines was H. Dobbs of London who was established there in 1803. During his career his firm name changed several times, and thus it is possible to gauge fairly well the date of his productions. Chronologically he was as follows: H. Dobbs, 1803-1816; Dobbs and Co., 1816-1836; H. Dobbs and Co., 1836-1846; Dobbs and Bailey, 1846-1851; after 1851, Dobbs and Kidd. He was also known as "Ornamental Stationer to the King." Queen Victoria used many of Dobbs' lace papers for programs for her entertainment at Windsor castle. Many fine valentines were also produced in France during this period. Two importers listed in the trade of importers of French goods in 1852 were Augustine Thierry and Edward Elliot of Buckesbury.

Soon high-class stationers realized a business in valentine manufacture and began to produce papers with narrow, embossed borders. By 1810, these borders, still remaining narrow, were not only embossed, but pierced through the paper. In the following years, borders increased in width, and in many instances real lace was copied. One such stationer was B. Sullman of London, who was one of the first firms to produce stationery decorated with embossed and die-stamped

chromolithographs. They quickly entered the valentine market in the 1820s and produced tiny valentines decorated with ribbons, silk medallions printed with valentine verses, and tiny chromos often elaborate with silver and gold trim.

Top: Fine laced valentine with tiny orange medallions. $85-100. *Bottom:* Red underlay with gold leafed lace overlay. $85-100.

Marked "B. Sulmann" in lower corner of lace. $75-90.

George Kershaw, established in 1824 as a bookseller and then as a stationer, made some very fine specimens. His work is known for its delicate workmanship, great variety of style, and beauty.

About 1825 an interesting innovation in the lithographed valentine appeared. This was the cobweb. The lithographed design of a flower or some sentimental scene was cut circular fashion or like a spider's web with a string and the tassel sewn to the center. When the tassel was pulled, the whole design lifted up, disclosing a second sentimental picture. Cobwebs continued in popularity through the 1860s. These were the forerunners of mechanical valentines, valentines which progressed toward more and more elaborations until openings revealed a considerable depth of scenes, or pulled tabs caused heads, arms and legs of characters displayed to go into various motions.

By the l830s one could purchase fine lace papers and decorative paste-ons from stationers, and with the aid of "Valentine Writers," people at home could write their own verses. These embossed papers were letter size with envelopes to match. Mansell was known as a "fancy stationer" in 1835 and was a licensee of George Baxter. He daintily outlined many of the delicate flowers in the lace borders which he produced, and at times he used colored backgrounds under the lace.

The mid-1800s records the exchange of the first valentines in America, and the best of the early handmade ones come from the Pennsylvanian Germans. Known for their handmade marriage, birth and baptismal certificates, their valentines are beautiful indeed. *Valentine Writer* in 1787, a necessary captivating little book, was filled with advice and helpful verses, for alas, all lovers are not poets. Valentines of the late 1700s were generally of the cutout type, made by folding a sheet of paper several times and then cutting through the folds with a sharp knife or scissors. Many of these early valentines were imported from England who provided great quantities of cards to her colonies and America.

In 1833, Elton & Company of New York City began printing valentines which were hand-colored and had no words, leaving room for the love-stricken sender to pour out his or her heart with personal sentiments. Edward P. Whaites, Thomas W. Strong, P. James Wrigley, Charles P. Huestis, T. Frere, and Pascal Donaldson were also early manufacturers of valentines, all of which were situated in New York City.

The chromolithographic process was brought to the United States by William Sharp in 1939 with Boston being the location for his business. The 1840s found the "mechanical" or "movable" valentine becoming more and more sophisticated. Figures, with joints held together by thread, were animated by moving a cardboard tongue. Another interesting fact to note is that it was in America that the "accordion" or "lift-up" which raises the lace paper above its foundation, was invented.

By the mid-1800s, New York City was the center of the valentine business with at least five firms established there, distributing to all the salesmen who sold three million valentines in 1857, amounting to over $250,000. These valentines ranged in price from three cents to thirty dollars. It was in this time period that a vast assortment of materials was used which included artificial flowers, beads, feathers, velvet, plush, silk lace, shells, cork, sachet and perfume, dried flowers and grasses, seaweed, net, straw baskets, spun glass, imitation precious stones, and even human hair. The use of tiny mirrors in the center panel, or a little lace-edged envelope surrounded by hand-painted flowers, was not at all uncommon.

Valentine flowers were not always painted, made of paper, or of muslin. Beautiful blooms contained on cards were sometimes made from feathers. In Brazil, gorgeous flowers were devised and executed from the feathers of exotic birds from the South American forests by nuns in convents. Marine flowers and even real hummingbirds were stuffed and boxed in tiny nests to carry sentimental messages in their beaks. Useful gifts were also incorporated into cards. A lace or pear-handled fan might be hidden beneath flowers, mottoes, and cupids. Ornamental hairpins, pin cushions, miniature bottles, lockets, watch trinkets, and even rings were listed as some of the "use articles" to be combined with appropriate poems.

In England, Clarissa King, working for her husband, Jonathan King Sr., designed and constructed such valentines as mentioned above. King is credited as being the first to put items such as glitter, tinsel, and feathers on valentines. She made one valentine for a special customer with 3,000 pieces attached. Not only was she creative, but she was fast in that she could assemble these elaborate valentines in half the time it took others. The Kings did so well that they quickly moved into more spacious quarters. Jonathan King Sr., died in 1869, leaving Jonathan, Jr., in charge. More women became involved in their business ventures as Jonathan, Jr. and his wife, Emily Elizabeth, opened a valentine shop, naming his wife as proprietor. Building their factory close to home helped their daughter, Ellen Rose King, supervise 30 women and girls who worked 11 hours a day assembling valentines by hand. The King valentine business continued to be successful until 1905 when Jonathan, Jr. retired.

Extremely fine lace with gold leafed eagle with verse inside on tiny chromo. $85-100.

Left: Elaborate lace with tiny chromos and red underlay. $100-110. *Right:* Gold fold down lady on gold leafed lace. $100-115.

Chapter IV
Latter Half of Golden Age:
1850-1899

Valentine manufacturing continued to be perfected in process and grow as an industry as countless Americans fueled this popular craze. Mechanization helped bring the chromolithographic business into modern times. In the late 1850s machinery was invented that made silhouetted forms possible. Cutting dies, which could be raised to a specified height before falling onto a printed sheet, punched away unwanted paper. The outlines of each figure were left, attached to each other by narrow ladders. These easily separated figures were referred to as "swags." Eventually, embossing and cutting dies were combined into one tool.

By 1863, the first steam-driven lithographic printing machine was patented, along with thin steel plates (replacing stones previously used). During this period of chromolithography, most scraps were comprised of 20 to 26 colors per design. Most of the production remained centered in Germany.

After printing the scrap, sheets went through two further distinct processes. The first, embossing, gave the sheets their raised three-dimensional appearance and multicrenellated surface. The initial machines which accomplished this task were "Swinging Weight" presses, which were counter-balanced presses that stamped a "male" die into the reverse side of the printed art work, stretching the paper slightly. All of the sheets were coated with a gelatin and gum film before they went through the embossing machine. This allowed the paper to stretch without cracking the printing ink, and gave the finished product a highly glazed sheen. Thus *Glanz Bilder* as a German term for these scraps becomes easier to understand.

From the embossing machine, the glazed and embossed sheets were transferred to the second process, the punching or stamping press. A cutting die was used to cut away all the surplus areas of paper from the design that had been printed leaving the images connected by small ladders which often bore the trademark of the manufacturing company. These stamping machines were individually operated by foot treadles.

Often manual laborers beat the paper to ensure that the excess paper was removed and that the finished scrap had a clean outline.

The most expensive scraps were those finished with gold leaf. The gilding technique was performed between the embossing and cutting process. A sheet of gold leaf was placed onto the scrap face. By using a heated brass die, the lacquer on the scrap was melted and fused the gold leaf onto the relief. These gold leafed scraps appeared on many early valentines and continued just into the start of World War I when this process became too expensive to duplicate.

Many of these scraps were used by American greeting card manufacturers on high quality paper produced in America, produced earlier than often thought. The first American mill was opened by the Rittenhouse family of Germantown, Pennsylvania, in 1690. Another paper-producing company was started by the Gilpin mill, also in Pennsylvania in 1787. Handmade "Laid" paper was manufactured from 100% rag fibers and was very durable. "Laid" paper means that the paper has evenly spaced parallel lines which are watermarked into the paper. "Wove" paper is handmade paper made on a mold in which the wires are so closely woven together that the finished sheet does not show any wire marks, Many of this early paper does have watermarks which will identify the mill in which it was made.

Extremely popular were the valentines which employed sheets of lace paper. Once perfected, lace paper made in England was the rage attracting the interest of many. One such person was Charles Dickens who inveigled his way into Raphael Tuck's firm to learn more about the art of producing paper lace. The writer that he was, he reported, "Engineering a mundane doorway and wiping feet on the cocoa mat of the earthy earth, I could not conceive of the realm of sublimated fancy which lay beyond. . . Would I step this way? I was shown how a plain sheet of paper was prepared for a lace-edged valentine." Dickens goes on to describe the intricate process of hand sculpting dies, engineering machinery, and orchestrating the cutting of the laces.

In the United States, American paper mills attempted to reproduce this lace, but only coarse, imprecise lace papers resulted. Thus, even spies were sent to England in an attempt to discover the closely guarded secrets of its production. One such spy was Jotham W. Taft who returned to the United States with drawings of the lace-making machines. Unfortunately, the results were far less than satisfactory. The machinery he had designed and produced, created perforations so ragged that the lace sheets could be only used for envelopes. But fortunately, this provided Americans with some very elaborate lacy envelopes, which later was the impetus for embossed envelopes which resembled lace. It would be years later that this art would be perfected.

Charles Goodall & Sons issued a series of cards in 1862, thus beginning general use. Some companies employed famous artists. Marcus Ward & Co. contracted with Kate Greenaway and Walter Crane, Messrs. De la Rue with William and Rebecca Coleman while Raphael Tuck & Co. employed Royal Academy artists. It should be noted that the valentine is one of the sources from which the Christmas card emerged. Some of the manufacturers added Christmas greetings to a design originally made for a valentine, thus economizing costs.

Gleason's Pictorial, a magazine that flourished from 1851 to 1859, printed an allegorical print of St. Valentine's Day as a valentine to its readers. A winged cupid conspiring with a prospective suitor enamored with the charms of his lady love combined with roses, birds, and a lute all were perennial symbols of this holiday. *Frank Leslie's Illustrated Newspaper*, a weekly of the late 1800s contained illustrations from the artist William Ludlow Sheppard, an American illustrator, who normally used Southern scenes as the background for his magazine illustrations. In the February 26, 1870 issue, his drawing depicts a young girl seated near the fireplace who has guessed incorrectly the beau who has sent her a valentine. The presumed sender is pleased while the real valentine, standing behind him, is understandably upset. *Godey's Lady Book* also contained many engravings featuring valentines.

Since postage rates were extremely high, small valentines were the most popular in the late 1850s, continuing into the 1860s, and into the early 1870s. By this time, valentines were specifically marketed for sending to relatives. Therefore, strictly sentimental proposals were placed inside of any such valentines. This shift provided a big boost to the commercial market. All of these trends caused small valentines to be the most popular since they could be sold in bulk, for families to send to everyone.

In 1856 Marcus Ward, a Belfast publisher, opened a London branch. Walter Crane designed cards for them and they were, of course, the leading publisher for Kate Greenaway, H. Stacy Marks, and Moyr Smith, an artist who also designed tiles for pottery firms. They quickly obtained a reputation for fabulous valentines. In 1897 the firm was awarded the Golden Medal of Victorian Era Exhibition, Earl's Court, for their exhibit of lithography and stationery.

De La Rue was another publisher who added valentines to their wider repertoire of printing and paper-goods manufacture. In the 1820s, when its founder, Thomas De La Rue from Guernsey, was still in charge, it made playing cards and disposable paper clothing in addition to valentines. It was Thomas De La Rue who discovered how to make the finest type of white, shiny-surfaced cards, adopted by many other manufacturers of valentines. Among their stable of artists were W. S. Coleman, J. M. Dealy, known for his portrayal of fetching children, and Ernest Griset, one of the most fanciful depicters of animals and birds.

In February 1875, *St. Nicholas* magazine mentions a London firm that featured 368 different valentines ranging in price from two cents to sixty dollars. Raphael Tuck was the company which this magazine profiled, reiterating some of the very fine valentines of different varieties being produced in that year. The magazine also documented the increasing popularity of sending valentines in the United States.

The most expensive valentines were a result of the fashion of the mid-1870s which combined a message with a useful gift. Perfume bottles, lockets, and rings were most often used. All of these were combined with appropriate poems. Music boxes hidden in gloves and handkerchief boxes were the ultimate in valentines as they played "Then you'll remember me" or some similar popular melody of that time period. Silk neckties, a smoking cap, or embroidered slippers were suggested as useful presents to be included in a gentleman's valentine.

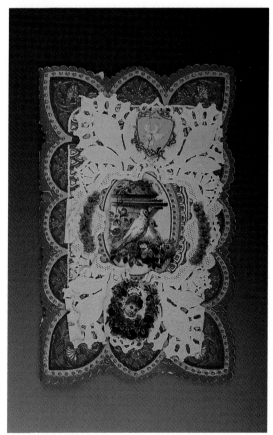

Elaborate, intricate lace which reveals turtle doves underneath and opens to hand-colored verse inside. $100-120.

In the late 1870s, lace sheets of paper were layered. At first some pieces were just laid on top, but towards the late 1870s, folded hinges to give valentines a 3-D effect as well as build up their layers were innovated. Wood & Meek of England manufactured many of these early lace sheets layered on valentines as well as A.T. Bullock and Sprague in the United States. These layered sheets of lace were used in a variety of ways. When used, much of the center material was used separately for trimming yet another valentine (usually smaller). In early stages of use, the piece was merely laid on top intact. Later the centers were removed and little chromos of children or a lady's head, was placed in the center. Sometimes a unique little scene was added to the base of the valentine and then a chromo head placed over that.

The chromos produced by Edward Elliot and Augustin Thierry revolutionized the valentine card market in England. Small corner scraps surround the main ornamented theme of the card and verses were subtly concealed within an arrangement of lacy gauzelike material. One popular theme used especially by the Dobbs company was flowers entwined around figures or surrounding hand-written verse. Sheets of reliefs complete with message verses were sold during the latter part of the l 9th century. Such greetings as "Truly Thine," "Forever My Love," or "Forget Me Not" were favorites. The relief was often hinged or glued in one corner so that when removed, it revealed the hidden verse. Some of the more popular verses included:

Oh! Might we never, never part,
But Live, and live so true;
The sign that rent thy constant heart
Should break my lover's too.

Little one! Pretty one!
Gentle as the dove;
May not one, to such a one,
Send a little love?

If others be as fair,
What are their chances to me,
I neither know nor care,
For thou art all to me.

Frame opens to lithographed image inside cover with simple three-line verse. $125-145.

Another type of valentine seldom seen is the wax valentines manufactured in the 1870s and 1880s. These were created in sports, patriotic, sentimental, religious, and children's themes. Usually made in hollow molds, and then hand colored, wax figures were often arranged on pink and white mountings such as satin. Drawn with threads, the satin swirled around the wax figure. The entire valentine was subsequently sprinkled with stars, figures, and mottoes with valentine sentiments. A few of these wax figures are then mounted on net and lace pillows, and placed against a fine embossed commercial mount. The sports series used a wax boat, the patriotic used a bust of President Grant, and the sentimental series used a white dove. The figures were molded in candy and cookie molds.

An 1876 catalog of chromos from Germany contained such categories as school girls, naughty boys, cupids, butterflies, and birds--all of which came by the sheet. In Germany these chromos or scraps were also known as *reliefbilder*, *relief*, *bokmarken*, *pressbilder*, or *andachtsbild*. French terms included *images*, *les chromos d 'enfance*, and *decoupure*. Several characteristics of this period can be found in cards. Layering in one fashion or another was characteristic of most types of lacy valentines, but the 1870s started with little sheets of lace merely placed on top so they would lift up at one end. During this decade manufacturers started using folded hinges to give these cards a three-dimensional effect. It is actually St. Valentine's Day that brought forth the great profusion of paper from Germany. In early

Left: Silver lace edge on which tiny chromos are attached with verse on tiny chromo inside. $120-135. *Right:* Tiny silk ribbons connected corners tied with knots, yellow rose chromos inside surrounded by verses. $120-135.

17th century Germany cut-paper tokens made for religious celebrations were similar to the "snowflakes" made by elementary students from squares of white paper, folded, and cut into designs. Gradually these religious tokens evolved into love tokens.

There were several factors which made commercial valentines so viable as a business venture. The pristine veneer of Victorian society in America and England forced amorous men and women to play cat-and-mouse courtship games. One of these courtship games included sending valentines to someone anonymously. Thus, many beautiful, elaborate valentines were sent in the hopes of gaining someone's attention. Secondly, economics was a factor in the beginning of the penny post in 1840s England. Previously, mail was expensive with the cost determined by mileage and paid for by the receiver, not the sender. Once computed by weight and paid for by the sender, mailing valentines became affordable for most people. Lastly, the invention of embossing

and cutting dies meant that parts for valentines could be manufactured by machine, paving the way for countless colored and varied examples for senders from which to choose. In America, it was extremely fashionable to not only send valentines, but to deliver them in person. In 1847 over three million valentines were sent in America, and it would be impossible to ascertain the number which were delivered in person to admiring lovers.

While most of our valentines were imported from England and Germany in this period, some Americans were beginning to see the profit potential in producing cards in America, taking advantage of such a popular custom. Early efforts often included using American paper and workers to assemble valentines using printed scraps from Europe. While there were many small companies and individuals involved in early valentine manufacturing, there are some significant manufacturers which need to be explored to understand America's role in card production.

American Valentine Manufacturers

Esther A. Howland

Esther A. Howland is a well-recognized and respected manufacturer of valentines in the United States. Her entry into this business is intriguing to chronicle. In 1849, Esther A. Howland of Worcester, Massachusetts, received a valentine. It had an elaborate border of fine lace paper and was decorated with colored flowers cut out and pasted on. In the center was a small pocket laced with green paper, within which was placed a small re-edged note containing the fervent sentiments appropriate to the season and the day. At this time her father and three brothers conducted a large stationery business. Graduating from Mount Holyoke Seminary the same year she received the valentine, Howland, who was so pleased with receiving her first valentine, determined to import a few of them from England. When they arrived, she quickly became convinced that she could improve them.

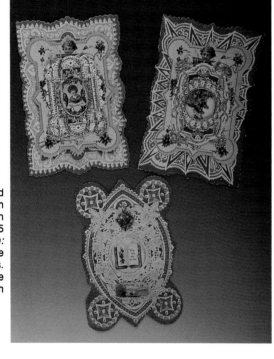

Top: Two layered valentines with tiny chromo in center. $85-95 each. *Bottom:* tiny simple lace with three layers. $80-100. All three are marked with red "H."

Procuring lace paper, colored paper, and paper flowers, she made two valentines. Pleased with the result, she made a dozen or more designs, and asked her brother, who traveled for the firm, to take the samples with him on his next trip and see if he could obtain orders for her. Upon his return, he surprised his sister by handing her orders amounting to five thousand dollars. Expecting only orders amounting to a hundred dollars or so, Miss Howland was, at first, skeptical about being able to meet production. Upon consultation with her brothers and father, however, it was decided the orders could be filled.

Embossed paper was ordered from England, and Mr. Howland went to New York to buy colored pictures from the only lithographer in this country. When the materials arrived, Miss Howland invited her friends to assist her. One cut out pictures and kept them sorted in boxes. Another, with models before her, made the background of the valentines, passing them to another who further worked on them. So they went from one hand to another until finally the last valentine called for in the orders was completed.

Assortment of marked Howland cards with intricate layers of lace, one upon another. marked "H." $85-110 each.

The second year the number of orders doubled, and so was the working force in the factory. In time, quantities of enameled colored pictures and other ornaments were imported from Germany; but as these had to be cut out with scissors, the enterprising woman had a set of dies made for that purpose. Howland then conceived the idea of embossing the little lithographic ornaments and wrote to the members of the firm in Germany telling them of her plan and that she would have the cutting dies made and sent to them at their expense. The idea was new and they wanted the credit of originating it, so they declined Miss Howland's offer and had the dies made in their own country. A few months later, embossed and cut pictures were on the market, but the onlyadvantage the originator of the plan received was in being able to buy them in the more convenient form. Miss Howland also tried, unsuccessfully, to duplicate European paper laces and scraps.

The fame of Howland's valentines spread all over the country, and the business increased so rapidly that in a few years Miss Howland was sending out more than one hundred thousand dollars' worth of cards. One firm in New York, which was using more than twenty-five thousand dollars' worth of her valentines, attempted to control her production. Unable to do that, they offered to buy the business out. That, too, failed. But Howland continued on. While the valentine business was in full swing, her cards attracted much attention because she added a lot of color to the available lace papers. She was the first one to place little colored seals to add color to the corners. Howland is also known for the paper spring, in which small pieces of paper were folded in an accordion style spring and placed under each layer of the card. Another novel idea was placing a colored paper wafer underneath the coarse paper lace, thereby creating a softening appearance.

Howland had a long table constructed so that her young workers could pass the valentines down the assembly lines. History records the fact that Howland was well respected and well liked by her employees, paying them very well. She continued to run the business out of the third floor of her home which contained a skylight until she reorganized her company into the New England Valentine Company in the 1870s and moved her operation a few blocks away. Howland's valentines are distinguished by the color-glazed paper she used behind the embossing to make the lace stand out. Disliking inscriptions on the outside of her cards, Howland often had verses printed on small slips and pasted inside the cards. It must be noted that her valentines were "put together by hand," not "handmade."

Unfortunately, Miss Howland met with an accident, falling on an icy sidewalk and injuring herself so that for years she was obliged to manage her business from a wheelchair. She continued her work until her father became ill

and required constant attention. The business was then purchased by several of her employees, one of whom is quite recognizable, Whitney. Howland's valentines are often identified by a small red "H" on the back of the card, a small white heart glued on the back of the card with the red "H" stamped in the middle of the heart, a tiny label with a red "H" stamped in the middle, or the initials "N.E.V.Co." used after that company was formed in the 1870s.

In 1850, *The Ladies' Own Fashionable Valentine Writer* was published to help Americans write effective verses for these early cards. The early black and white cards were colored by the assembly line method with each worker armed with one color and passing them along. Verses were added by the sender of the card. The prices paid for valentines bothered the editor of *Godey's* who deplored the sums of money young men were spending on flimsy paper tokens. "He might be much better," she said, "to send to the lady of his heart, a subscription to *Godey Magazine* and could obtain a three year's subscription for the price of one valentine." In 1857 over three million valentines were sold in the United States, retailing from three cents to thirty dollars a piece. By the end of the 1850s America was producing them in large quantities and began to realize that it was not successful to import from England since the taste of the two countries differed.

Right: High quality assortment of Howland cards which were on high end of market due to five layers and use of many chromos, all marked "H." $100-120 each.

Large example of marked Howland valentine, red "H" in right back top corner of card. $100-125.

Raphael Tuck

Raphael Tuck is another important figure in the valentine card business who created highly collectible cards, with offices later established in the United States. Tuck moved to England where he first started selling hand-framed pictures, and later on, oleographs, chromolithographs, and black and white lithography. Ultimately he founded the corporation, Raphael Tuck & Sons, Ltd. Publishers to their Majesties, the King and Queen of England and Her Majesty Queen Alexandra, Tuck was one of the most prolific publishers at the turn of the century. Tuck had offices in London, Paris, Berlin, Toronto, and New York. New York's office was established in 1885 at 298 Broadway.

Raphael Tuck was born in 1821 and died in 1900 before he saw the runaway expansion of his business with the postcard's and valentine's card's popularity. Tuck's aim was to produce merchandise for every taste and choices of designs for every price range. While designing and editing were accomplished in the London offices, the printing was done in Tuck's fatherland, Germany. Tuck became a British citizen in 1875 and was appointed publisher to Queen Victoria in recognition of his craftsmanship and design. In 1882, he retired and turned the business over to his three sons. Prior to 1882, the company was Raphael Tuck and Company. After 1882, it was known as Raphael Tuck and Sons.

Tuck's fame also lies in the fact he hired the best designers possible. For example, in 1881, J. C. Horsley was invited to Tuck to design Christmas cards featuring children. As early as 1880 Tuck sponsored competitions with money prizes to obtain new designers. An unbelievable number of Valentine postcards and cards were produced over the years. While Tuck's valentines displayed great craftsmanship and design, it must be noted that he was a volume publisher. Therefore, the label itself does not automatically make it valuable.

Early assortment of fold-out cards richly decorated with lace chromos attributed to Raphael Tuck. $80-90.

Early assortment of square cards approximately 5" X 5" all richly decorated and attributed to Raphael Tuck in his early years of business. $75-90.

Louis Prang

Another well-recognized name among valentine cards is Louis Prang. Better known for his Christmas cards than for his valentines (in fact, he is considered by many to be the "father of the modern day Christmas card"), Prang moved to the suburbs of Boston, Massachusetts. There, under the name L. Prang and Company, he reproduced paintings in color with so much skill that today it is quite difficult for the untrained eye to detect the differences between his copies and the original. He is known for his advanced process of lithography whereby he could print twenty-four colors. His career ran from 1874 to 1890. Prang is known for the so-called "Prang method of education," which was a system to awake and develop the creative impulse in the young and one which he spent considerable time and large sums of money. Most of his work not only has his name but also the date in microscopic print in a line at the bottom of his cards. His contributions to lithography and the art which resulted in some marvelous valentines began early.

Prang's youth was abundant with design and bright with color because his father had owned a calico factory in Breslau, Germany, now Worclaw, Poland. Prang was a sickly child, so he frequently missed school. While absent, he often followed his father around the factory, taking in the details of color mixing, printing, and dyeing. He reached manhood just in time to become enveloped into the liberal revolutions sweeping Europe in the late 1840s. When those revolutions failed, he, like so many Germans, went into exile. Prang's destination was the United States, and after five weeks at sea, he arrived in New York City. Prang's first job was for Frank Leslie,

Silk fringed Prang card, double sided with Victorian flower theme. $45-60.

the publisher. Prang attempted many occupations, but gradually concentrated on lithography in color. Prints had been created in three or four colors, but Prang felt that much better results could be obtained. By the mid-1860s he knew enough to begin.

Prang displayed his first attempts at the Vienna exhibition of 1873 and publicized his display by handing out business cards chromolithographed with flowers. Some of the most elegant valentines of this period were produced by Prang starting in 1874. As is often the case with excellence, Prang's cards were relatively expensive. In Prang's method of printing, employees separated the colors and made a zinc plate of each one with hairline accuracy. The zinc plate was a change from previously used lithographic stone. Prang

said of his new method to *Chicago Lithographer and Printer*, "I have used zinc plates for nearly all my color plates since 1873, and I am positive that I have saved thereby fifty thousand dollars."

In a card with 28 colors it would take the artist three or four months to complete the 28 plates. Artists who worked for Prang included O. E. Whitney, Rosina Emmet, Elihu Vedder, Will H. Low, Thomas Moran, and Henry Sandham. Unfortunately the American market was being saturated with countless inexpensive German-printed cards, and Prang was unable to compete since he insisted on not compromising his quality. Gradually Prang's cards declined in number, unable to attract Americans more interested in price than quality in valentine's greetings. Prang's death in 1909 ended a magnificent career which produced all sorts of greeting cards.

It was in the December, 1884 issue of *Wide Awake Magazine* that M. E. Hollingsworth told of his visit to the Prang Printing company to see how greeting cards were produced. Hollingsworth met not only Louis Prang, but Maude Humphrey who designed cards for Prang. Prang showed them a book which contained the color separations for a card currently being produced. He tells of seeing "a stone on which was printed all the pale yellow parts of the picture, the fourth showing pale blue fitted in with the pale yellow," and so on. The artists' quarters was a long room lighted with many windows, looking out on blue skies, green trees, and cooled by rows of automated fans. By each of these windows sat an artist at work with pen and ink upon a zinc plate copying the image. The entire process was observed with the final question asked of Prang, "How can I recognize a Prang card," Louis Prang's answer was, "Your critical judgment will help you out; still people say there is a character to our cards of originality, freedom, and thoroughness which stamps them 'Prang's' without need of reference to the firm's imprint."

Extremely elaborate designed Prang card which sold for fifty cents. $75-90.

McLoughlin Brothers

A fourth name associated with valentines, especially comic valentines popular from the 1840s and well into the early 1900s, was McLoughlin Brothers. While McLoughlin Brothers is primarily known for children's books and games, this firm was also responsible for some superb valentine postcards at the turn of the century for a brief few years. Readily recognizable from their logo of a flying Mother Goose astride a duck, all of the McLoughlin cards were original illustrations used in other publishing areas during the 1890s. Similar to Tuck and other prolific publishers, McLoughlin Brothers used their illustrations countless times over many years. However, it must be noted, that it was a case of constantly borrowing from a stockpile created during the firm's golden years to help it survive the dual problems of mismanagement and stiff competition.

Its history started in 1819, when an immigrant from Scotland, John McLoughlin, arrived in this country seeking employment as a coach maker. Not finding employment in this area, he went to work for the Sterling Iron Company in New York City. There he met Robert Hoe, a manufacturer of printing presses. The men became good friends with McLoughlin developing a keen interest in the printing business.

Garnering all the knowledge he could, McLoughlin was hired by the *New York Times*, but his job soon ended when the newspaper ran low on operating funds. McLoughlin was not one to give up. He opened his own print shop in 1828 where he wrote and printed numerous pamphlets. Due to a depression in our country in 1839, he was forced to merge his new business with John Elton's. For the next eight years, the company was known as "Elton and Company." Both partners retired in 1848 and the business was taken over by McLoughlin's two sons, Edmund and John, Jr. Their hard work, publishing expertise, and marketing strategies soon produced a highly successful operation. Their success led to a new factory in Brooklyn in 1868. By the late 1880s, McLoughlin Brothers, in spite of stiff competition, was the largest firm in its industry. Some of their greatest artists included Thomas Nast, Palmer Cox, and Howard Pyle.

Edmund retired in 1885. In 1894 their business was so great that a complete, modern lithographic division second to none anywhere in the world was in full operation in the country. Twenty-two years after Edmund's retirement, John McLoughlin, Jr. died and the respected old company passed into the hands of John's two sons, James and Charles, who unfortunately had little interest in the daily operation of this company. Quickly McLoughlin brothers lost their prominence in the printing field. In 1920, Milton Bradley purchased the firm and moved the operations to Springfield, Massachusetts, and used the name for two more decades.

Early McLoughlin cards all marked "Mc L" on backs. $45-65.

Left: "Token of Love" opens up as well as entire card opens with magnificent long verse inside flap. $70-85. *Right:* Bust of little Victorian boy with elaborate lace, marked "McLoughlin" on back of card. $65-80.

George C. Whitney

The fifth well-known producer of valentines in this time period was George C. Whitney, who produced countless lace-style valentines from this time well into the 1930s. Among Esther Howland's employees was young George C. Whitney, who went off to fight with the 55th Massachusetts Volunteers during the Civil War, then returned and formed his own company with his brother Edward. In 1869 Edward broke away to form his own stationery business and George turned out valentines, taking over the old firm of Berlin & Jones.

In addition to George and Edward, there was a third brother, Sumner, who first farmed, and later taught school in Norfolk, Virginia. Returning to Worcester, Massachusetts, he involved himself in the valentine manufacturing business like his two brothers. His wife, Lura Clark Whitney carried on the business after his death in 1858. Edward associated himself with Sumner. They advertised under the name "The Whitney Valentine Co."

After they separated, Edward and George remained very close. Even though they were in competition, they never failed to remember that they were brothers. Of course, we remember George C. Whitney when it comes to valentines because George produced countless cards while his brother Edward was more involved in the stationery business. Whitney imported scrap from Germany and lace from England for his cards until 1874, when he moved into larger quarters and installed his own embossing machines.

One innovation occurred during Whitney's early career. In the 1880s, Americans finally discovered the secret to producing paper lace quite like the fine, intricate paper lace manufactured in Europe. American paper had traditionally been made of wood pulp, but only paper of a high rag content could sustain the clean-cut delicate incisions necessary to produce fine lace. Thus Americans could now rely on their own manufacturing firms to produce lace. George C. Whitney took advantage of this innovation, producing hundreds of thousands of valentines employing some extremely well-done American lace paper.

Fabric lace embellished center of framed chromo of gentleman offering his lover some flowers, marked with blue "W" on back. $85-95.

Silk ribbons and fabric lace surround bust of lady with love verse inside, marked with blue "W" on back. $90-100.

Whitney's success led to the purchase of A. J. Fisher Company of New York, who was among the first to produce comic valentines in the United States. When Whitney purchased the company, the Fisher Company had thousands of dollars' worth of cuts and plates for its valentines. Since Whitney despised comic valentines, he disposed of the plates. Oral history tells the story that Whitney sold the cuts and plates to McLoughlin Brothers secretly while telling those in the trade that he disposed of them as junk.

His most important acquisition was Berlin & Jones since this firm was among the oldest companies producing valentines. Thus he acquired vast amounts of materials, knowledge, artistry, and know-how which he quickly put to use in building a company whose name more than any other in the United States became associated with the word "valentine." Whitney's verses came from across America as creative freelance writers interested in making a "fortune" sent him samples. In fact, historic folklore records the post office being extremely upset with Whitney due to the volume of mail he received from individuals with valentine verses.

Whitney's cards closely resemble those of Howland except that his are marked with a small red "W" and later a small blue "W" stamped on the back. His business continued up to 1942, when the restrictions brought on by World War II closed it down.

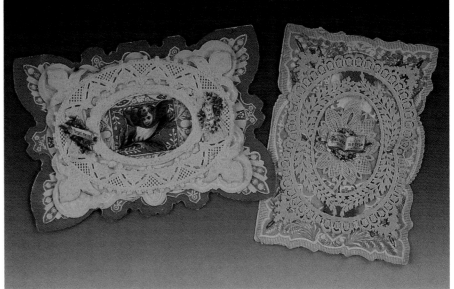

Left: Layer lace, marked with blue "W" on back, sold for ½ cent. $75-85. *Right:* Thin lace layer over lithographed fold-over, marked blue "W" on back, sold for ½ cent. $75-90.

Early assortment of Whitney produced cards which incorporated lace and chromos, red "H" on backs. $65-80 each.

Larger Whitney cards with red "H" on backs. $65-75.

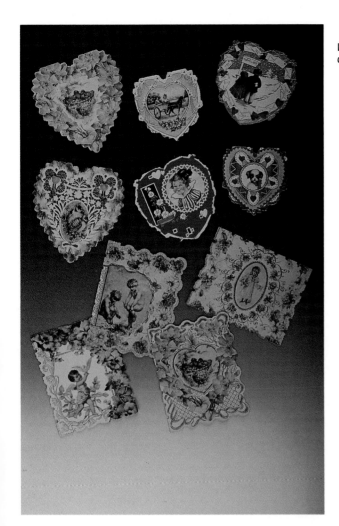

Large assortment of late 1890s Whitney cards. $20-40 each.

Elaborate square-shaped Whitney cards with red "H" on backs of all. $65-75.

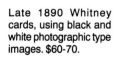

Late 1890 Whitney cards, using black and white photographic type images. $60-70.

George Gibson

The sixth and last not often well-recognized early maker of valentines was George Gibson. Gibson greeting cards' history actually started in 1850 when George Gibson and his family emigrated to the United States from Scotland, where Gibson and his family had operated a lithographic and copper-plate engraving business. Arriving in this country with a small French-made lithographic press, Gibson, his wife, and family eventually settled in St. Louis, where one of his five sons found work with a canal system that led him to Cincinnati. His three brothers followed and together they went into business using the small press. In 1850, the Gibson brothers, Stephen (34), Robert (18), George (14), and Samuel (12) founded Gibson & Company, Lithographers.

At first they printed bonds, stock certificates, business cards, and labels. Rather than purchasing goods to sell in retail stores, they printed their own goods such as patriotically decorated stationery, Civil War prints, honor and reward cards for schools and Sunday schools, and valentine novelties which were marketed through stationery, novelty, and art stores.

In the 1870s, the Gibson brothers began "jobbing" other artists' products such as Currier and Ives prints. They also jobbed imported German lithographed Christmas cards and oversaw production of the first American line of valentine greeting cards developed by L. Prang & Co. in about 1866. Five years later, Prang had achieved sales of five million such cards a year, and the Gibson brothers were soon designing and making their own line of valentines.

In 1883, Robert Gibson, the business manager of the four, purchased his brothers' interest in the company, becoming the sole owner of the company until his death two years later. His will dictated that the company was to be incorporated as the Gibson Art Company, with shares distributed equally to his four children: Charles, Arabella, William, and Edwin.

In the 1890s valentines were of the same general type. They consisted of a double sheet, the top of which was heavy or coarsely embossed in color, with the verse and valentine message printed inside. The more expensive cards had a cover consisting of two or more layers of lace and chromolithographs. These valentines were the traditional cards like those produced in earlier decades and were sold for five to ten cents each.

However, some changes did occur due to fierce competition from manufacturers all vying for part of the valentine card market. While the sending of valentines had declined in England, the custom in America was flourishing. In the latter part of this period, cards, sometimes single or folded in two, were often edged with all sorts of colored silk fringes, the folded cards usually having silk cords or tassels to help open the card. All of the leading manufacturers soon produced cards of this sort due to their popularity. Fold-over cards as large as eight by eleven inches appeared due to the fact that materials were more inexpensive and the process more refined so that such cards could be produced at a low cost, and be more available for sale. Lots of layers of colors, scraps,

and fancy work continued to attract the eye of those who wished to send traditional cards as first manufactured in the early 1850s. However, there was a refinement of what was previously known as the mechanical valentine. This refinement caused an entire new wave of styles as Americans quickly became enamored with these new innovations.

Three-Dimensional Cards Captivate Americans

If there is one card which attracts collectors' interests, it is the three-dimensional fold-out (mechanical in nature) valentine produced for many years. The earliest were produced in Germany and England, with Germany quickly capturing the American market with countless examples ranging in size from two inches to cards which exceed fourteen inches in height and width. Prices ranged from five cents to one dollar. Their scarcity lies in the fact that they were manufactured from inexpensive pasteboard (layers of thin paper glued together) and numerous layers held together by thin paper tabs which quickly broke and became unglued. Once broken, many of them were discarded. Many others were just simply discarded soon after Valentine's Day.

German mechanical, pull-down card with silk ribbon tab. $35-45.

Fold-outs from the 1890s to the early 1900s consisting of four or more layers of heavy paper board ingeniously connected by pull-like hinges are very desirable today. When pulled gently forward from the base, these creations assume a three-dimensional stand-up position. These multi-layered valentines, with the layers hinged by carefully camouflaged tabs, varied widely in format and theme. Nevertheless, they were most always sentimental in theme. Pink-cheeked cherubs nestled among pillows of satin and lace, holding baskets of lilacs; lovers gazed limpidly at one another from garden bowers, or glided among nameless waterways on garlanded and ribboned sailing vessels, or somewhat later, in open touring cars. In prime condition, the larger types are a spectacle to behold when displayed. Often too large, and actually almost too fragile to send safely through the mail, most were simply slipped into plain, unadorned envelopes and hand delivered. Until the start of World War I, these creations actually revitalized an industry which was waning.

Often times, the fold-out valentines were preserved and placed on parlor tables. But the majority of them were glued into albums due to the fad for albums which swept Europe and America in the 1870s after the Civil War. Scrapbooks arrived in the late 1860s around the same time that the mass production of scraps had started in Germany and provided a convenient way to see and handle these beautiful cards. The very first scrapbooks were more like notebooks, small and fairly indistinguishable from any other blank book. Gradually these albums became highly decorative, often rivaling the valentines contained inside the albums. These scrapbooks saved many large cards from destruction.

The Victorians loved flowers, attested by the appearance of blooms on almost every valentine manufactured. The rose was especially suited to the romantic theme of valentines. Rosebuds, tea roses, and cabbage roses appeared singly or in bouquets adorning valentines in baskets, wheelbarrows, and with birds, hearts, and hands. Other flowers commonly used in valentines included pansies, violets, lilies of the valley, lilacs, and even orchids. Embossing gave these flowers a very realistic quality.

English mechanical, 2" X 8" pull-down card with tabs which reveals intricate garden scene. $95-120.

Other than flowers, children, cupids and women often now appeared on valentines. Children appeared alone with other children in natural settings with adults, and dressed in every conceivable form of attire. All these scraps conformed to the Victorian idea of beauty: flawless porcelain complexions, tiny noses, rosebud mouths, huge and heavily lashed eyes, and thick heads of hair.

"Germany" or "Made in Germany" are usually the only identifying marks on many of these fold-out valentines. No matter where they were designed, where they were eventually sold, or whose trademark they might sometimes possess; these cards were printed in a German factory. The greatest number of these manufacturers were located in Berlin, although other German cities--including Hamburg, Breslau, Leipzig, Dresden, and Frankfurt--also housed valentine and other card manufacturers. However, one major firm, Emmanuel Heller, was based in Vienna.

Numerous single pieces of scraps were required to produce these very large, elaborate valentines. In an effort to save money in a period where so many scraps were needed for card manufacturing, publishers designed sheets in such a way to minimize the amount of tool making. By placing a larger number of scraps in a single sheet and increasing the size of the sheet slightly, they saved much effort and money. After printing and embossing, the scraps were separated into 1000 sheet swags, for wholesale distribution. The degree of complexity involved in the printing and manufacturing determined the final price.

Originally, these cards entered America via importers who often purchased paper goods. However, as the demand for these cards increased, German companies found it profitable to set up offices in the United States, particularly New York City. U.S. Firms which imported materials included George C. Whitney, Louis Prang, Dennison Manufacturing Co., and the Hebrew Publishing Co. Many of the early German printers were Jewish and it might seem strange that they be involved in valentines. But this company's involvement is easy to understand. Their popular Jewish New Year's cards often were changed slightly and used as valentines, thus gaining a large portion of the market. Some valentines were marked and these include those made by Ernest Nister & Co., the largest lithographic establishment in Germany, based in Nuremberg. Some English manufacturers who often marked their cards were the Artistic Lithographic Co. (1891-1914) who was operated by the Obpacher Brothers and Davidson Brothers (1883-1912) which produced both cards and valentine greeting booklets.

Siegmund Hildesheimer and Company of Germany specialized in early fold-out cards. An 1884 advertisement in *The Stationery Trades Journal* boasted of "Valentines, Tasteful in Conception." With offices in London, Manchester, and New York, this prestigious firm produced quantities of fold-out and other three-dimensional valentines. Unfortunately none of their valentines were marked, but their distinctive large, dimensional fold-outs with themes of transportation are attributed to this company through oral historians who have interviewed workers.

Rich embossed gold backing incorporated in 5" X 11" marked "German" pull-down. $45-60.

Elaborate card with heavy cardboard covers, pull-down with boy and girl, 3" X 4". $45-60.

Two examples of superb craftsmanship in heavy cardboard fold-downs, both which incorporate angels. $100-110 each.

Fold-down Coronation-type carriage with large quantity of doves, 11 ½" X 14 ¼". $165-180.

Heavily embossed back, 6" X 10", marked Tuck. $60-80.

Five-layer pull-down with honeycomb, 6 X 8". $50-60.

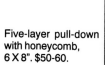

Heavy cardboard with deeply embossed flowers, 3" X 4" pull-down with pink carnations. $50-60.

Two early uses of Dresden foil trim used in front gates of heavily embossed paper layers. $65-75.

Six-layer card, 7" X 11", with profusion of flowers incorporating rich honeycomb fans on sides. $65-75.

Seven-layer pull-down, 7" X 9", with heavy lithographed cardboard. $75-85.

Georgian style, 8" X 9" pull-down, marked "Germany" 1887. $100-120.

Country girl fold-down with typical cardboard verse on lower right. $35-45.

Early fold-outs with heavy cardboard backs, which are open-laced and intricately printed. $20-30.

German ½ cent cards, 2" X 3". $5-10.

Six-layer basket-theme card, 7" X 10", with daisy sprays cut in relief on cardboard back. $85-100.

English valentine, 6" X 8 ¾", with profusion of flowers and detailed landscape on back cardboard. $75-85.

Early Dresden basket of flowers with six layers of flowers emanating from basket. $125-140.

Exquisite, fragile fold-out with silk ribbon, 3" X 3". $55-65.

Early use of red honeycomb in heavy cardboard backed pull-down. $50-60.

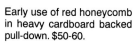

Raphael Tuck signed card with seven pull-down layers (back doubled as backing for Christmas card), 5" X 10". $60-75.

30

A Glimpse at Major Artists and Their Contributions

While it is impossible to mention all the early 1800s artists who were involved in providing art for valentines, it is important to document some of the great figures. Many artists were never identified because they were extremely talented, yet anonymous individuals who worked day after day providing beautiful illustrations, then went home to their families. In addition, many artists did not feel it significant enough to sign their work for various printers since many of them were merely "moonlighting" on the side and did not consider this temporary work to be of any real significance. Lastly, many manufacturers of cards did not deem it appropriate for artists to sign their work since the illustration was more important than the fame of a single individual who provided inspiration for these cards.

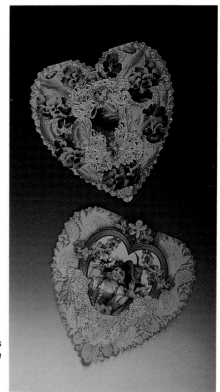

Two heart shapes designed by Kate Greenaway. $40-50.

Kate Greenaway

Born in England in 1846, Kate Greenaway designed and wrote verses for valentines. Greenaway was the daughter of a well known engraver for the *Illustrated London News* and also a cousin of Richard Dadd, of fairyland and patricide fame. Even while at her first school in Clerken, she began designing valentines for publishers such as Kronheim & Co. (1870-1871). Much of her work had a charming innocence, particularly appealing to John Ruskin, who in 1883 delivered an Oxford lecture on her work, and who wrote to her after receiving a card from her in 1880, "Luck go with you, pretty lass. To my mind it is a greater thing than Raphael's St. Cecilia." The Greenaway-type valentine, popular in the late 1800s, usually pictured children and lacy borders. Greenaway designed most of her cards for Marcus Ward and Company. Greenaway and Walter Crane also illustrated a valentine book *The Quiver of Love*, for Marcus Ward and Co. Her designs are not signed, so they can only be identified by comparison with her work in her picture books. She died in Hempstead in 1901.

Left: Card designed by Kate Greenaway, outside cover, 4" X 5". $95-110.

Above: Inside card with Greenaway designed print.

Frances Brundage

Frances Brundage was born on June 28, 1854, to the Rembrandt Lockwood family, in Newark, New Jersey. Her father, an engraver and architect, left his family when Frances was a teenager. Brundage earned money creating drawings and prints for Louisa May Alcott. With many books to her credit, it was not until Brundage was 32 years old that she married William Tyson Brundage, a painter. They were well suited for each other and at first, even signed their illustrations "Will and Frances Brundage." Some of her earliest work was for Raphael Tuck; their relationship lasted from 1900 to 1910 when she left to work for the Samuel Gabriel Company of New York, New York. Her marvelous portrayal of children, depicting the antics of boys and girls with absolutely delightful faces, enchanted Americans at that time. While she is well known for her postcards, her large valentines produced by Raphael Tuck are among the finest to be collected today. Enjoying a prolific career, Frances Brundage was 82 when she died.

Artist signed "Frances Brundage." $50-60.

Brundage designed for Raphael Tuck. $45-55 each.

Brundage designed for Samuel Gabriel Company. $150-175.

Brundage designed for Raphael Tuck. $45-50.

Chapter V
Romance Continues to Entice:
1900-1909

The Victorian era was very much still alive in America and that influence is reflected in valentines produced and sent during this decade. "Excess" and lots of decorative detailing were reflected in not only cards, but the elaborate customs evolving from a genteel life, full of proper etiquette. The events surrounding the exchange of these cards and parties held on St. Valentine's Day are of great interest. Many educational and women's magazines continued to provide ideas for party games, decorations, and refreshments. And once in a while, some interesting customs were recorded on the pages of various magazines. In 1908, *St. Nicholas* chronicles some fashions of this decade in Valentine's Day parties. Carolyn Wells, author, condenses her "The Story of Betty" as originally published. Betty's friend, Jeanette Porter, had no dress to wear to the winter reception, always a very important event in this small community. Betty offers to buy a dress for Jeanette who is of poor financial means but Jeanette's pride prevents this from occurring. Since it was February 10th, Betty devises a plan with her mother. Betty plots to purchase a dress and put it in a Valentine's box, "with lace paper around, and sorts of hearts and darts and things, and a verse, lovely, loving verse." After picking out a dress, Betty and her mother go to another store to purchase valentine cards for Betty's friends, including Jeanette.

Once home, Betty fashions a decorated box, inside which she places the dress and copies on the blank page of a real valentine, the following verse,

"To Jeanette from St. Valentine—

On Cupid's Day
One may, they say,
Send tokens to a friend,
Of love most true,
As mine for you,
A love that ne'er shall end.

Accept then dear,
The token here,
That tells this love of mine;
Or else a dart
Will pierce the heart
Of your fond Valentine."

On Saturday, February 14th, a messenger is sent with the valentine and the boxed dress. At four o'clock, a group of about a dozen or so youngsters gather at Betty's house for a Valentine's party to show off valentines. Jeanette arrives "positively gay" and announces at the party that she is going to the reception. "Oh, I had a dress for a valentine! The loveliest dress you ever saw! It's just a dream!," she exclaimed. When questioned about the sender, Jeanette replies, "You see, I'm not supposed to know who sends a valentine. If I were to know, it would take away all the joy." Betty's own joy in the gift was the pleasure she had afforded her friend in this very charming story.

Valentine Greetings Proliferate as the Industrial Age Evolves

American firms continued to produce valentines which, by the start of World War I, would be necessary if such greetings were to continue during war times when European goods were no longer available. George C. Whitney continued to produce numerous valentines. From 393 Main Street in Worcester, Massachusetts, Whitney expanded to the Taylor Building at 184 Front Street. The building soon was too small, and another story was added. While there, the firm was incorporated as the "George C. Whitney Co." with George as President. Still expanding, they moved to 67 Union Street where a disastrous fire destroyed the factory on January 12, 1910. At that time they had over two hundred thousand dollars in stock and one hundred thousand dollars in machinery, all of which were lost. Fortunately, almost all of the valentine stock had already been sent out. Two days later, a temporary roof was put over part of the remaining building and 75 men went quickly back to work. Once rebuilt, the company employed 450 workers and occupied some 75,000 square feet of floor space. Other companies got their start in this decade as well: Buzza, Gibson, Rust Craft, and Vollard. Their history is more ingrained in the next decade, and is therefore detailed in the following chapter.

In 1906 *Scientific American* in its February 17th issue, chronicled the work of a New York firm (McLoughlin Brothers) producing valentines for the American market. Germany, though it did not recognize the holiday, supplied many of the cards and novelties used in our country. It should be noted that Germany, a country which was one of the major suppliers of valentines, never did get involved in the celebration of St. Valentine's Day. This is an interesting fact considering that the scrap and cards produced were often created for Christmas, the customs of which were deeply rooted in German society. By this time, Americans were producing a large number of cards, many of which were assembled from German-made and printed materials. As well as producing valentines, the United States exported large quantities to all parts of the world.

A paper lace-making machine worked year-round to meet the enormous demands. Three principal types of valentines were produced: the comic, the old-fashioned lace, and the "novelty" valentines, the latter being the most expensive. The comics, extremely popular in the early 1900s, were photo-engraved and printed in the usual manner.

Special machines, however, were involved in producing lace valentines. The lace-making machine consisted of two rolls, one a die, and the other a matrix of the desired design. A wider paper ribbon passed between the rolls and was cut by them. A brush bore against the matrix roll, leaning off all adhering bits of paper, and another brush which bore against the ribbon removed the cuttings from the lace. The paper was chalked before entering the rolls to prevent the lace from sticking to them and tearing. This lace paper was fastened with paper hinges to the embossed cards. The hinges, them-

selves, were made by a small hand-operated machine, which creased long strips of paper by folding them in and out like camera bellows. From these strips the hinges were cut off as desired.

The cards to which the lace patterns were attached were printed in large sheets with an attractive design, after which they were embossed. These embossed sheets were passed on to the folding table, where they were folded in sets of three, and then fed into the cutting machine. This machine was provided with cutters of various design, which cut out the

McLoughlin heavily laced cards, 5" X 6". $35-45 each.

cards with scalloped edges. Then the hinged lace frames were glued on, thus forming the familiar old-fashioned lace valentine, a perennial favorite of traditionalists who shunned modern styles.

One modern design was a card with various celluloid and/or parchment attachments or ornaments. Invariably these cards had easel backs so they could be placed on shelves or tables, doubling as room decorations long after St. Valentine's Day had passed. Sizes varied considerably with the largest being about 14" in height and the smallest about 3". Most were dimensional with layers which presented a most stunning effect when displayed. The ornaments, cut out by hand with a punch and maul, were then attached to the cards by means of a simple riveting machine. The small brass rivets were carried in a cup at the top of the machine, and were fed down into a channel by the notched wheel which could be seen near the upper end of the machine. At the bottom of the channel was an escapement which, at each operation of the machine, released a rivet and let it drop down under the riveting hammer. Thus these valentines were quite inexpensively produced.

McLoughlin laced cards, 6" X 6". $40-50.

Below: Closed 3" X 3" intricate lace card with chromo, McLoughlin. $30-40.

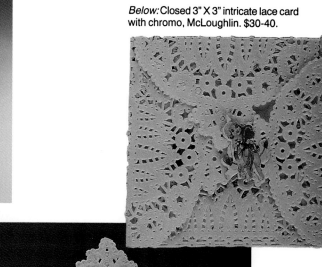

Very fine examples of McLoughlin cards, riveted with various parchment attachments and silk tassels. $20-30 each.

Left: Open McLoughlin card revealing chromo.

Right: Two examples of McLoughlin, riveted cards with chromos, both with easel backs. $35-45.

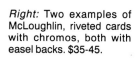

McLoughlin, riveted parchment in Art Nouveau style in pastel colors. $50-60.

McLoughlin, riveted heart card with easel back, very intricately colored and designed. $50-65.

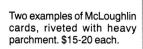

Two examples of McLoughlin cards, riveted with heavy parchment. $15-20 each.

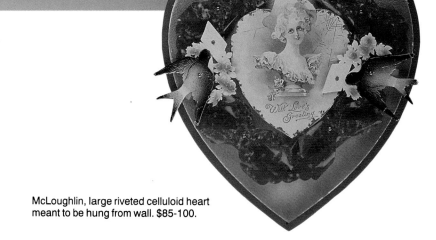

McLoughlin, large riveted celluloid heart meant to be hung from wall. $85-100.

McLoughlin, riveted with celluloid flaps. $30-35.

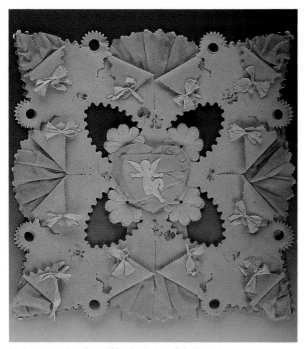

Unknown valentine with riveted celluloid and parchment with ribbons, easel backed. $20-25.

McLoughlin mandolin incorporating both celluloid and parchment with ribbons and chromos. $150-165.

The more expensive novelty valentines were made up with silk and satin puffs and bows of ribbon which had to be applied by hand to the cards. The only machine work done on these cards was the printing of the colored design and the blocking out of the cards. The rapidity and neatness with which the puffs and shirred borders of the various designs were manufactured was remarkable. In making a heart, for example, hot glue was lightly applied to the card along the outline of the heart. Then the puff was made from a semicircle of silk, the edges being gathered as they were pressed into the glue by drawing and puckering them with the fingernail. The borders were made of two pieces of cardboard cut to the proper curve and covered with colored silk, which was lapped over the cardboard and glued to the underside. This silk was gathered as the edges were glued down, and the border pieces were glued over the edges of the puff. In a similar manner many apparently intricate and elaborate designs were simply produced.

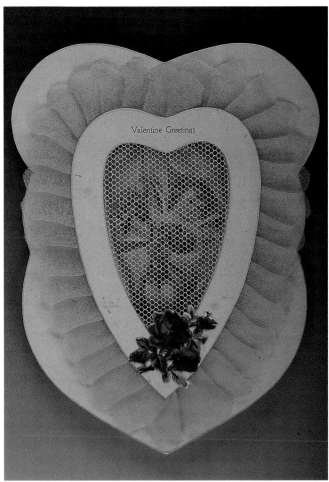

Attributed to McLoughlin, with rivets and pink lace netting which reveals chromo of angel. $50-60.

Circular May pole theme card, 5" X 8", with heavy cardboard and extremely delicate honeycomb. $120-140.

Valentine themes such as transportation (cars, trains, and later planes), comic personalities (Foxy Grandpa, Buster Brown, and The Yellow Kid) and other images emerged as new innovations and traditions were started in the United States, offering a social history. Continuing in popularity were the three-dimensional fold-outs from Germany. Produced by the thousands, they began to use paper honeycomb tissue along with the layers of design.

The incorporation of honeycomb tissue was one new addition appearing more and more on valentines in this era. Honeycomb tissue, sheets of colorful tissue paper, glued, and folded flat were produced by German manufacturers in an attempt to give their valentines new appeal in a time of stiff competition. When it opened, it appeared as the cells of a bee's honeycomb. While red was the most familiar color in a later decade, pale pinks, greens, and blues are characteristic of this period when Victorians were so interested in nature. The interest in nature led card manufacturers to duplicate as much as possible, not only the colors of nature but the designs as well. Thus the profusion of flowers, lush garden scenes, and cottage walls rambling with roses are the principal design themes on so many valentines.

Above: Circular honeycomb card with trellis, 6" X 8". $50-60.

Above: Two flower themed honeycomb flower pot cards. $35-40 each.

Left: Honeycomb valentine, 5" X 8", rare due to three honeycomb colors and Dresden sails and railings. $110-120.

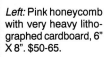

Left: Pink honeycomb with very heavy lithographed cardboard, 6" X 8". $50-65.

Right: Pink and pale green fountain with lithographed girl to side, 8" X 11", rare large example. $85-100.

One of the more popular themes for valentines at the turn of the century was the automobile, or the "horseless carriage" as it was referred to. Artists of the period delighted in using the newest invention to hit the American market as a topic for valentines. While there was much resistance to the horseless carriage, it was nevertheless the topic of conversations. Most feared the automobile. What is most intriguing is the fact that while valentines were promoting greetings via the horseless carriage, there were only in the neighborhood of 8000 cars in the country and less than 150 miles of paved roads. However, 1908 changed all of that with the appearance of Henry Ford's automobile plant which successfully turned out the Model T. It was then that even more automobile-themed cards hit the market.

The most revered valentines were the extremely large, often up to 14-inches in height, fold-out valentines often hand delivered to the recipients because they were far too fragile to trust to the U.S. mail. In addition, since these were the costliest of all cards, the sender often wanted to be present as the elaborate card was unfolded to reveal its unrivaled beauty. Manufacturers of the late 1800s continued to turn out valentines, each one more dazzling than the ones produced the previous year. It was important for them to attract the same "high spenders" of the previous year in an attempt to top the card purchased last year. There was a strong market for large valentines, in an era which now promoted sending cards rather than presents on St. Valentine's Day.

Most of these were very rarely marked by the manufacturer's trademark, but rather marked "Germany." Part of the problem in identifying such cards by manufacturer is the fact that designs and themes were "borrowed," or better said "pirated" by companies. As a result, one signed zeppelin card adorned with Victorian children manufactured by Prang or Tuck in 1900 might appear the next year on the market with the generic "Germany" trademark. However, subtle changes in colors and positioning of the items were often used to avoid criticism of copying.

Rare transportation car pull-down, 6" X 7", intricate paper wheels and deeply embossed. $250-275.

Above: Extremely rare, 3" X 5", fold-out car with easel type bottom, marked "Raphael Tuck." $275-300.

Left: Touring car with honeycomb, 6" X 16", extremely embossed with great detail. $125-140.

Two 7" X 9" sailing ships marked "Germany" sold as matching set. $130-150 each.

Fold-down sailing ship with honeycomb, 7" X 10". $160-175.

Fold-down sail boat, 6" X 8", marked "Raphael Tuck." $100-110.

Elaborately embossed ship with tissue see-through sails and intricate trim, 11" X 13". $90-100.

Companion boat with above photo, meant also to be sold as set. $90-100.

Elaborate wall-designed card with blue honeycomb, 12" X 14", marked with patent date "1904." $125-135.

Intricate trellis in seven-layer pull-down, 7" X 11". $75-90.

Pull-down, 7" X 11", rare in that it incorporates silk strings to connect doves. $95-100.

Medium sized fold-downs, 4" X 6", marked "Germany." $25-30.

Medium sized fold-downs, 4" X 5", marked "Germany." $40-45.

Above: Simple pull-down with violets and lilies of the valley, 3" X 6". $35-40.

Left: Tuck signed heavily embossed, 4" X 7", thick cardboard. $45-50.

More common "German" valentines, 4" X 5". $10-15 each.

Heavily embossed cardboard, 4" X 6", with carefully lithographed figures. $20-30.

Bowl of cherries, 7" X 9", rare subject material. $65-75.

Above: End of century 2" X 3" pull-downs, "Germany." $5-7.

Left: Common pull-downs, 3" X 4", marked "Germany". $10-15.

Above: Rare 5" X 8" Dresden trimmed valentine with die-cut tree as background. $50-65.

Right: Pull-down, 7" X 10", with boy holding flower pot, marked "Prang." $60-70.

Below: Assortment of common German pull-downs, 2" X 3". $3-5 each.

Above: Inexpensive 2" X 3" German-printed, ½ cents each. $5-10 each.

Above: Common pull-downs, 3" X 4", marked "Germany". $10-15 each.

Another extremely popular valentine was the booklet. These sometimes humorous, most often sentimental booklets were for the special people in one's life. While postcards of this period lacked intimacy and privacy, these valentine booklets afforded an opportunity for the sender to add personal sentiments and verses to the printed text.

Basically, the booklets are small, hard, cardboard-cover books with a sentimental message illustrated by lithographs. Often a single poem by a leading poet made up the whole of the message, but some booklets contained excerpts from different poems by one author. Longfellow, Tennyson, Kippling and Whittier were favorites at the turn of the century. The most common size for these valentine greeting booklets was 5 by 7 inches. Sixteen pages including the title page and cover is the maximum length of such booklets, although most contain 10 pages or less. Leading the field were Cupples and Leon Co. of New York. The Berger Publishing Co. of Buffalo, New York, did copyright their booklets in 1907, and along with Holiday Publishing Co. of New York, produced greeting booklets with Henry Longfellow's poems. Charles E. Graham & Co. of New York was primarily responsible for the long slender (8 1/4 by 3 1/4 inches) valentine booklets.

A large number of these greeting booklets also included handsome little books with more text, but with the same general intent. Two companies who produced such booklets include Ideal Book Builders of Chicago and the Garman Company. One company to produce these booklets and actually term them valentine's booklets was Collins of Glasgow and London. They tapped an impressive talent bank from Shakespeare to Omar Khayyan. Since these booklets were intended for someone special, they were not as common as the fold-out three dimensional valentines or lace valentines still being produced.

Another popular variation on the booklet were the enveloped plain flat cards and folders tied with ribbon, with decorated designs on the front. Inside one would find a thin fold-over piece of delicate paper held in place with a tassel or ribbon. Printed on this fragile paper would be a valentine verse often with an intricate black and white lithograph. Albert M. Davis of Boston pioneered this type of valentine. First importing cards from England and Germany, he soon entered into the production business himself. The A.M. Davis Co. prospered for many years until ill health forced him to liquidate his business.

Above: Assorted greeting booklets from Art Lithographic Publishing Co. of New York, Bergman's of New York, and Ernest Nister. $20-25 each.

Above: Card booklet with four inside pages, marked "Germany." $10-15.

Left: Greeting booklet with series of valentines poems inside, marked "Raphael Tuck." $5-10.

Art Nouveau type air-brushed card booklets, marked "Germany." $5-10.

Above: Booklets, 2" X 5", each with six pages of verses and black and white lithographs, USA. $5-10 each.

Right: Booklet with 12 pages of verses and lithographed art, 3" X 5", copyright 1910 by Hays Lithographing Co. of Buffalo, NY. $20-25.

One very popular theme of greeting booklets and valentines of this period was Art Nouveau. *Art Nouveau* is a French term meaning new art, thought of as modern, but adapted from older styles and art forms. Much was derived from Gothic and Rococo. Valentines of this period took their motifs and patterns from nature and were often carried out with unrestrained exuberance. Flowing curvilinear lines were another characteristic of these cards. Irises, pansies, and violets with leaves and stems which curled and intertwined in long, flowing designs were favorites. Also popular were white or cream colored fold-over cards featuring voluptuous women with long flowing hair intertwined with flowers. Art Nouveau particularly appealed to Raphael Tuck and the International Art Company. By the end of this decade, Art Nouveau declined and cards soon lost this design theme.

Right: Art Nouveau cards, chromolithographed design on front, verse on back (do not open-single sheet). $2-4 each.

Above: Art Nouveau heart, signed "Whitney." $25-30.

Francis Brundage, Art Nouveau themed cards. $10-12 each.

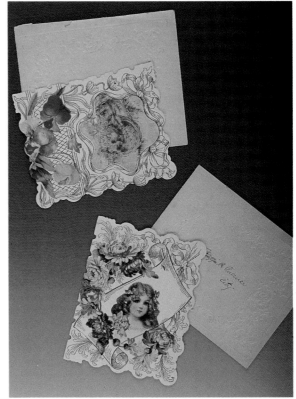

Art Nouveau cards, German. $5-7 each.

Art Nouveau cards. $5-10 each.

Assortment of German cards, Art Nouveau. $5-10 each.

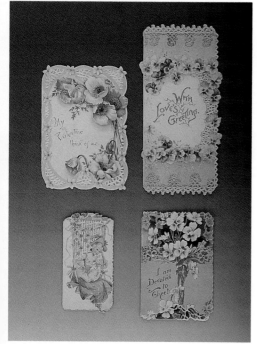

Art Nouveau cards, heavy cardboard stock, marked "Raphael Tuck" on back. $2-3 each.

Art Nouveau cards attributed to Louis Prang. $10-12 each.

Art Nouveau flat cards, design on front and verse on back. $2-3 each.

Above and Right: Simple inexpensive Art Nouveau flower-design cards, marked "Germany." $1-2 each.

Above: Art Nouveau flats with verses on back, 2" X 3", marked "Germany." $2-3 each.

Turn of century assortment c cards, Art Nouveau. $5-7 each

Right: Art Nouveau cards by Raphael Tuck, 2" X 3", designed in England and printed in Bavaria. $3-5 each.

Above: Assortment of simple Art Nouveau flats with verses on back of some. $1-2 each.

Left and Below: Art Nouveau cards Ernest Nister. $5-7 each.

Left: Cards of various manufacturers all illustrating Art Nouveau designs, 3" X 5". $5-7.

Below: Art Nouveau flats with verses on back, American. $2-3 each.

Above: Two simple cards by Raphael Tuck in Art Nouveau style, air-brushed. $2-3 each.

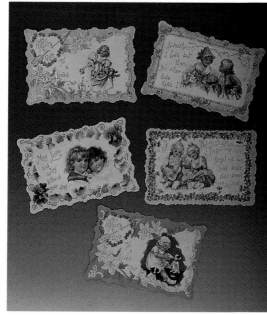

Right: Flats with Art Nouveau designs on front and verses on back, 3" X 5". $3-5.

Fan, marked "Germany." $150-200.

Two other popular novelties appeared in this decade. Fans printed on heavy cardboard stock and joined with thread or silk ribbon were popular with all age groups as women found them both utilitarian and artistic. In fact, their use as fans to cool oneself in the hot summer air contributed to their extreme scarcity today. Most of these fans were designed by artists who today go unrecognized as their work was not signed. Upon examination, however, many artist's designs can be recognized by style and colors. Chromolithographed fans, especially those in sections (held together by threads or ribbon) which individually form the fan when extended, are almost impossible to locate and are a treasure for any collector who comes across such a novelty. While many of the fans are not labeled, close examination can many times reveal the artist and manufacturer by comparing signed valentines with these unsigned fans.

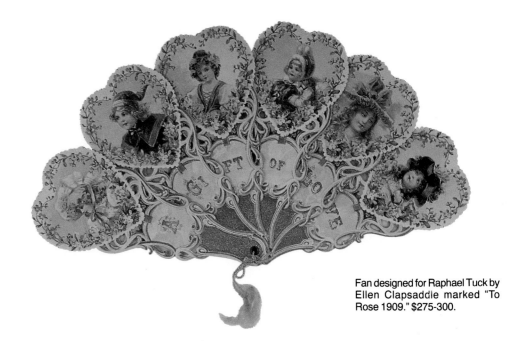

Fan designed for Raphael Tuck by
Ellen Clapsaddle marked "To
Rose 1909." $275-300.

Fan designed by Samuel L.
Schmucker for Winsch. $285-310.

Another popular novelty of this period were hanging valentines, often referred to as *drops*. Collectors refer to hanging valentines as *charms* if they contain one to two separate layers joined together or made to hang by means of a small ribbon loop at the top. *Drops* are those which consist of three or more separate parts attached together.

Manufacturers took a series of graduated valentine pieces arranged from large to small, glued ribbon or silk thread to the back of each piece, then covered the backs with tiny thin paper medallions or stars. The earliest of these types of valentines were heavily embossed and printed on thick cardboard stock. Those made in later years were rarely embossed and usually printed on thin paper. When assembled, these valentines were meant to be hung as a decoration in windows or on the walls in Victorian parlors and bedrooms. The most desirable valentines for collectors are the ones which consist of four or more layers and those which are artist signed. However, any *drop valentine* in good condition is desirable as most were discarded because the colors faded from hanging for a year or more in the open light.

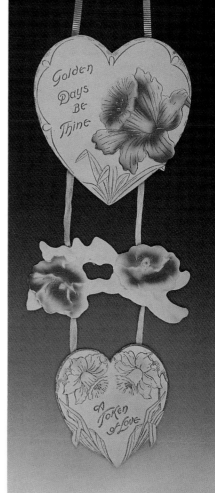

Left: Art Nouveau air-brushed drop by Louis Prang. $50-60.

Left: Elegant drop lithographed on heavy stock and marked Raphael Tuck on back top heart piece. $45-60.

Right: Drop designed by McLoughlin of New York. $25-30.

Above: Drop marked "Germany" on back. $5-10.

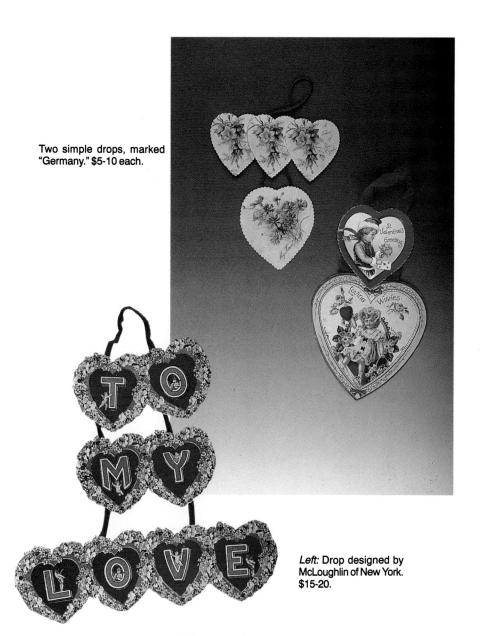

Two simple drops, marked "Germany." $5-10 each.

Left: Drop designed by McLoughlin of New York. $15-20.

Schmucker designed for Winsch. $75-100.

Extremely elegant depictions of cherubs and children, marked "International Art Co." on backs. $20-25 each.

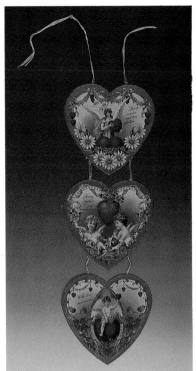

Left: Drop designed by International Art of New York. $50-60.

Right: Rare leather tooled drop, handpainted. $30-40.

Above: Bear with mechanical arms and legs, marked Raphael Tuck. $85-100.

Above: Very rare and unusual drop with fold out flower vases, and greeting heart card at bottom, Germany. $75-85.

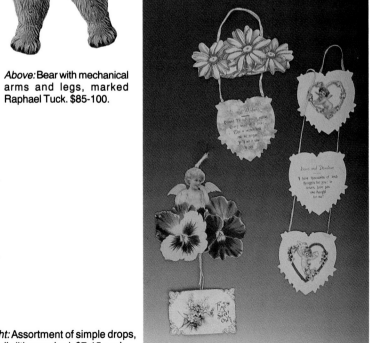

Right: Assortment of simple drops, heavily lithographed. $7-15 each.

Left: Drop designed by McLoughlin of New York. $35-40.

Above: Drop with satin, 10" X 16", silver trim, and deeply embossed flowers. $25-30.

Right: Drop with greeting card booklet as last layer. $15-20.

Above, Left and Right: Two drops, marked "Germany" on backs of both. *Left:* $5. *Right:* $15-20.

Postcards continued to be popular in America since they were relatively inexpensive. European and American manufacturers capitalized on this trend by producing hundreds of thousands of different cards, starting in this decade. Combined with the fact that the postage was cheaper, many Americans opted to send postcards rather than the costlier postage on traditional card valentines. Many different artists were employed to design these cards. It would be impossible to detail them all, but some are important to note because they designed both postcards and valentine cards for the American market.

Rose O'Neil

Kewpie valentines are very desirable cards as they reflect the imagination and creativity of Rose Cecil O'Neil, born in 1874, in Wilkes Barre, Pennsylvania, the oldest of six children. Never an exceptional provider to his family, her father William moved the family to Nebraska. Earning an art award in Omaha, Nebraska, at the age of 13, she started a career which took her to New York City in 1893, where she studied art for three years and did illustrations for many magazines including *Harpers Weekly, Harpers Bazaar, Truth,* and *Harpers Monthly.* While she was in New York, her father moved the family once again, this time to the Ozark Mountains of Missouri. In 1904, her novel *The Lady in the White Veil* was published. In 1909, O'Neil began doing illustrations for *Ladies Home Journal* who quickly accepted her elf-like "kewpies." In 1910 they appeared in *Woman's Home Companion* and the following year her book *The Kewpies and Dottie Darling* was published. Her kewpies appeared in 1914 in *Good Housekeeping Magazine* and a Kewpieville series appeared in the 1925 issue of *Ladies Home Journal.*

Gibson Art Company introduced the first Kewpie postcards in 1915 and produced about 65 different cards, sometimes using the same borders in various sets. Many of these were, of course, valentines. Her signature is found on all Gibson Art cards. Campbell Art Company published the easel-style cards in a series entitled "Klever Kards." Each has a partial cut on the outline which is made to fold down and the card can be stood up easel-style. Most of these are numbered from #210 to #753 on front of the card and signed or printed "After Rose O'Neill." Valentines which copied this style were also produced as cards. One very elegant card was illustrated with Kewpies in a boat, one of which is holding a little wooden oar. This card makes an excellent display piece with its easel back.

From 1912-1914, O'Neil stayed in Europe. With the war coming, she and her sister Callistra moved to Washington Square in New York City. In 1925, the two sisters again moved to Carabas Castle, near Westport, Connecticut. Eventually, in 1936, O'Neill retired to Bonniebrook, Missouri. Here is where

Above: Kewpie postcards and cards from Germany and United States. $15-25.

Left: Kewpie "Klever Card" designed by O'Neil. $25-35.

Kewpie "look alike" from Germany. $10-12.

she found true happiness, writing her autobiography. Rose O'Neill died in 1944 and is buried in the family cemetery at Bonniebrook with her mother, brothers, and sister. In 1967, the International Rose O'Neill Club was founded by Pearl Hodges in Bransom, Missouri in her memory.

Grace Drayton

Viola Grace Gebbie was born in Darby, Pennsylvania, on October 14, 1877. Having had a father who was a successful art book publisher, Grace drew from an early age. Her drawings of children often depicted on valentines were actually perfected from early childhood self portraits. When Grace was in her teens, her father died, causing a family financial crisis. At 17, she accepted professional art assignments to support her family. At 22 she married Theodore E. Wiederseim, Jr. In 1904, she began her 20 year relationship with Campbell's Soup Company. In 1911 she divorced her first husband, and married Heyward Drayton III. Thus her work could be signed "Grace Gebbie," "G.G. Wiederseim," or "GG Drayton." Grace is known for her Dolly Dingle character. By December 1933, she fell into poverty having lost her job with King Features Syndicates and died three years later on January 31, 1936, of a heart attack.

Grace Drayton designed mechanicals, USA. $15-20 each.

Grace Drayton designed stand-up for Bergman. $10-15.

Grace Drayton designed mechanicals, USA. $20-25.

Grace Drayton designed stand-up for Bergman. $15-20.

Ellen Clapsaddle

Ellen Clapsaddle is one of the most prolific designers of postcards, with almost 2300 designs credited to her. While she is best known as an illustrator, she also created portraits and landscape work, and taught china painting in her home town of Richfield Springs, New York. First educated in rural schools, Clapsaddle attended Richfield Springs Seminary from which she graduated in 1882. After Richfield, Clapsaddle attended the Cooper Institute in New York City for two years where she developed her artistic talents. In 1885, she returned to South Columbia where she painted china. In 1898, Ellen and her mother traveled to Europe at the expense of the International Art Publishing Company. Clapsaddle's mother died in 1905 and Ellen moved to New York City.

Most of her work on postcards, including those of valentine themes, was done in the 1906-1914 era for International Art Company which had offices in New York and Berlin. She also did do some artistic work for Wolf Bros, Tuck, Stewart & Wolff, J.M. Jackson & Son, and Hammond Pub.Co. Her cards for International Art were often used for other types of paper items for that firm, such as the easel-back valentine. Many of her designs incorporating children were often found as cutouts for standup valentines after they had been originally issued as postcards.

Unfortunately her career ended somewhat tragically as she had invested all her funds in International Art Co. and lost it all when war broke out in Germany in 1914. Clapsaddle was in Germany when World War I began and returned to the United States soon after. She died penniless in 1939 in New York City. Her friends paid for her funeral.

Ellen Clapsaddle designed valentine of unusual subject material for Raphael Tuck. $130-150.

62

Ellen Clapsaddle flat stand-up for International Art Co. $30-35.

Above: Ellen Clapsaddle designed honeycomb stand-ups, richly detailed children. *Left:* $60-70. *Right:* $45-55.

Left: Ellen Clapsaddle designed honeycomb stand-up for Raphael Tuck. $65-75.

Ellen Clapsaddle designed
for Raphael Tuck. *Left:*
$10-15. *Right:* $25-30.

Ellen Clapsaddle designed
postcards for Raphael Tuck and
International Art Co. $10-15 each.

Later Ellen Clapsaddle designed
valentine from1923. $45-55.

Ellen Clapsaddle designed stand-
ups of high quality for Raphael Tuck.
Left: $25-30. *Right:* $30-35.

Katherine Gassaway

Katherine Gassaway designed many postcards used on valentines by Raphael Tuck, National Art Company, and Ullman Manufacturing company. Gassaway designed cards from 1906-1909, with most of her work unsigned. Her drawings of children are known for their huge expressive eyes and very round faces. In fact, her work is often compared to Clapsaddle.

Katherine Gassaway designed for National Art Co. $10-15 each.

Katherine Gassaway designed for Raphael Tuck. $45-60.

Assortment of valentines all designed by Katherine Gassaway for Raphael Tuck. *Airplane:* $85-95. *Others:* $15-30 each.

Chloe Preston

Born in Bishopthorpe, Yorkshire, England, and educated at home, Chloe Preston become recognized world wide for *The Chunkies' Adventures* and *The Peek-A-Book Gardeners* both of which were printed in 1921. Her Peek-A-Boo characters appeared on many valentines and are distinguished by their enormous round eyes and long eye lashes, many times all around the eye. Preston's valentines primarily date to the World War I era. Many of her illustrated and designed valentines have bright red honeycomb tissue paper worked into their designs. Ranging in size from 4 to 12 inches tall, they are free-standing with easel backs.

Chloe Preston designed mechanicals, Germany and United States. $5-10 each.

Fold-out honeycomb, 9" X 12", designed by Chloe Preston, Germany. $75-85.

Fold-out honeycomb, 12" X 10", with Chloe Preston design printed on heavy cardboard stock. $60-70

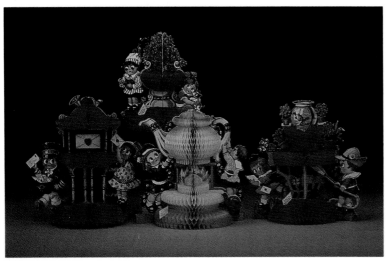

Chloe Preston designed children with large eyes and thick eyelashes, Germany. $55-65 each.

Chloe Preston designed children in large valentines with deep colors and rich, red honeycomb, Germany. $45-60 each.

Jason Frexias

Working for the John Winsch Publishing Company of New York, Jason Frexias produced a great number of valentine postcards, the designs of which were often also used for other types of valentines. Frexias created the baby-faced children used on Winsch's valentines while Samuel L. Schmucker created the women used on the cards. Collectors often comment on the use of the same design for different holidays. Many of the designs Frexias created for one holiday were lifted, transposed, and changed for other holidays. For example, the same yellow-bonneted child might appear on an egg for Easter, a pumpkin for Halloween, and on a heart for Valentine's Day. Frexias and his portrayal of children is often seen, especially in German fold-outs created just before World War I, since numerous European printers "lifted" or "borrowed" his caricatures for their cards.

Jason Frexias type designs following his rendition of children and cherubs. $5-10 each.

Jason Frexias signed fold-down valentine. $30-35.

R. F. Outcault

One intriguing illustrator of valentines was Richard Felton Outcault, who was born on January 14, 1863 in Lancaster, Ohio. Coming from a wealthy family, he was a freelance artist for *Life, Judge, Truth*, and the *New York World*. For the *World*, he produced a series of cartoons to be printed in color, Hogan 's Alley, which featured a small bald child in a yellow night shirt. The Yellow Kid did appear on valentine post-cards as well as on valentine cards themselves. Another even more popular figure to appear on valentines was Buster Brown created by Outcault in 1902. Buster Brown's balance between hellraising and propriety was a healthy boy dressed in a proper fashion. Buster Brown and Tige, his dog, appeared on postcards and valentines alike. He is easily distinguished by his hat and blue clothing finished with a dapper bowtie.

Buster Brown valentine designed by R.F. Outcault. $40-50.

Children stand-ups designed by R.F. Outcault. $15-20 each.

Rare early comics designed and signed by R.F.Outcault in 1903 for Raphael Tuck. $50-60 each.

H. B. Griggs

H. B. Griggs is one of the most intriguing artists of this time period in that no one really knows if Griggs is a male or female. Regardless, Griggs illustrated cards for Valentine's Day. Most of this artist's work was done for one publisher, Leubrie and Elkus of New York. Printed in Germany, the cards were extremely successful and thus Leubrie and Elkus put Griggs under exclusive contract. The earliest cards appeared in 1907. There are over 500 signed Griggs cards alone, with hundreds of others not signed. With the beginning of the war, many publishers including L & E lost their businesses, because all of the production work was done in Germany.

John O. Winsch

One very recognizable manufacturer of valentine postcards was John O. Winsch of Stapleton, New York. Winsch first issued postcards in 1910, shortly after the passage of the Payne Aldrich Act, which increased tariffs on imported cards. His cards were printed in Germany and imported into the United States for distribution. While the common price for cards was one cent each, Winsch priced his cards at two for five cents. Winsch reached its peak in 1911, but continued in business until 1915. During his short time, Winsch copyrighted over 3000 designs.

Above: John O. Winsch marked valentine postcards. $15-30 each.

Left: Valentines with applied gold metal attachments, some of which were designed by Winsch. $15-35 each.

Comic Valentines

There is an entire category of valentines often ignored since they are quite different from the traditional cards sent. Comic valentines often ridiculed or poked fun, in varying degrees of subtlety and good taste, at the concept of romantic love. The so-termed "cruel" valentines were often sent for the express purpose of slighting the recipient, in a spirit of malice or spite. Often these were sent after lovers had quarreled or had recently broken up before Valentine's Day. This allowed people who disliked somebody to say often anonymously what they did not have the courage to say to that person's face. We must also recall that in the early years of the U.S. Postal service, the recipient, rather than the sender, paid for the delivery. Thus it is quite plausible that the sending of these comic valentines might have helped to revise this system of payment. For it must have been a double insult to not only receive such a card, but then be expected to pay the postman to receive it.

A. Park of London was an early maker of comic valentines. Printed on gaudy paper, they were meant to be folded and enclosed in an envelope for mailing. Only the makers were sorry to see the appeal of these dwindle away. Some of them were A. J. Fisher; Elton & Co.; Thos. Strong; Charles P. Huestis; Charles Magnus; and McLoughlin Brothers of the United States, as well as Raphael Tuck & Sons, Ltd. London. The Tuck valentines are the most sought after by collectors today.

John McLoughlin was the "daddy" of the American comic valentine according to many historians. His father came from Scotland in the 1820s, and in time John began to take an interest in the family print shop in New York. The shop had some rough wood cuts from which were struck hideous little figures in black and white, decorated with occasional blobs of flat color, pictures now worthy of any collector's attention. In the 1870s, John established a profitable side line in hate using these caricatures. It proved to be a field just big enough for a single firm, so that during his life, whenever another company ventured in the field, McLoughlin cut his prices in half until the interloper succumbed. McLoughlin himself harbored no malice, for it is documented that he actually had parts of Mother Goose rewritten before he would reprint them.

The majority of the drawings on McLoughlin's desk were by Charles Howard who conceived and drew almost all the comic valentines produced in America between 1880 and 1910. During his lifetime over twenty million of these ugly caricatures, with their garish blots of color and unkind doggerel verses were sold annually, and it has been estimated that the total number sold in all (they were reprinted year after year for several more decades) was well over a billion. Howard received $2.50 for each of his drawings used by McLoughlin.

The beginnings of these statistics started in the late 1870s when John McLoughlin was firmly establishing America's largest manufacturing company of children's books and toys. Extremely popular in England, comic valentines were manufactured in the United States, but in very small quantities. McLoughlin brothers and Charles Howard turned comic valentines into a business employing over 300 workers year-round. Towards the end of the 18th century, the old "comics" had become so abusive and lewd in England that St. Valentine's Day itself had almost fallen into disfavor. But Howard brought a new respect to this art form, creating many examples of clever caricature and humor of a high order. Indeed, some of his later series have a wittiness that reveals a true insight into human nature.

In 1903 Howard was quoted as "Yes, I make nearly all the comic valentines in this country, or rather I design them. But it's the public's fault, not mine. Several times I've tried to give them serious, pretty pictures. And once I persuaded my publishers to try some not so undignified in the way of a series of 'don'ts,'

Earliest of C.J. Howard's valentines for McLoughlin in 1890s. $15-20 each.

but the public wouldn't have them. . ." Howard made a fortune from his monstrosities, but towards the end of his career he seemed ashamed of them. His earliest designs are signed in full—"C. J. Howard," but through the years he used just "C.J.H." and finally just "H," or nothing at all. He had always dreamed of illustrating children's books, but never fully realized his ambition. His name was so firmly linked with the comic valentines that the few book illustrations he created were done anonymously.

Howard experimented with many varieties of comic valentines. Some series were narrow sheets nearly two feet long, others were done in small format as postcards. But almost all of his drawings can be identified by his characteristic "H" in one corner. He lampooned to perfection the vain, the greedy, the mean, the foolish—every known weakness in human personality. He had an uncanny ability to depict a type in such a way as to make the beholder wonder if it was a human-looking animal or an animalistic person.

Not all of Howard's comics are ugly or vicious. His "New Woman" series, circa 1890, is a delightful spoof of that fad. His masterpiece, however, is his "Hall of Fame" series done around 1905. These twenty-odd caricatures, depicted as statuary busts in architectural niches, are as choice a collection of human frailties as seen anywhere. One sharp-nosed female, tagged "Mischief Maker" has inscribed below her niche "The Champion in Her Line." Howard delighted in visual puns. One of the "Hall of Fame" comics shows a ne'er-do-well whose bust rests upon a pedestal, the base of which is completely obscured by a cloud. The caption: "Without Visible Means of Support." In the older comic valentines, artists poked fun at the butcher, the baker, and the candlestick maker. Charles Howard lambasted not only these, but the bicycle addict, the card-shark, and the new-rich social climber as well.

If one compares various printings of a single design, some interesting details can be noted. Some of Howard's

Earliest of C.J. Howard's valentines for McLoughlin in 1890s. $15-20 each.

earliest comics were crudely stencil-colored, or the color was achieved by wood-block printing. As the designs were issued from year to year, the successive improvements in color printing can be easily seen. The later reprints (1920s) are generally distinguishable from the old by the added embellishments of hearts, etc. and the "Printed in U.S.A." imprint at the bottom.

Howard's comic valentines enjoyed an interesting longevity. Drawings first issued in 1880 were still in print when he designed his last series in 1910, and were still printed in the 1920s and 1930s. In fact, some of his hardy perennials were found in dime stores in the early 1940s. W. J. Rigney, who excelled in writing jingles, wrote almost all the verses on Howard's valentines. Rigney was a mild, easy-going, studious man. He lived a double life in that his major interest was the writing of rhymes of childhood and simple, lucid prose.

George Fox directed the business of producing comic valentines in the mid-1920s with over six million of them sold in 1926 alone. According to Fox, "We—those 6,000,000 of us—enjoy sending the 'comics' because we are so civilized. No longer can we 'say it with a club' in the old-fashioned way." Fox went on to detail the fact that comic valentines were a method to vent jealousy, malice, and hate.

Earliest of C.J. Howard's valentines for McLoughlin in 1890s. $15-20 each.

Earliest examples of C.J. Howard's valentines for McLoughlin in 1890s. $15-20 each.

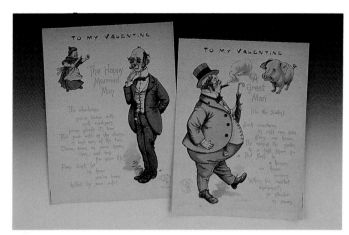

Early 1900s C.J. Howard's valentines with
Goose McLoughlin trademark. $10-15 each.

Early 1900s C.J. Howard's valentines with
Goose McLoughlin trademark. $10-15 each.

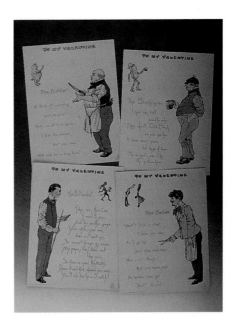

Raphael Tuck comics, copyrighted
1902. $10-15 each.

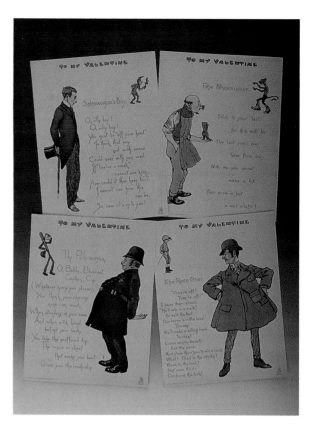

Raphael Tuck comics,
copyrighted 1902. $10-15
each.

Honeycomb zeppelin with deeply embossed detail, 8" X 6", Raphael Tuck. $130-150.

Chapter VI
European Cards Shine: 1910-1919

This was a decade of change brought about by world events which were to affect the lives of countless Americans. World War I changed the card market in 1914 when European imports all but disappeared. Even though chromos and elaborately crafted valentines were not to disappear entirely, their elegance was marred during war times. During the war, women were brought into the workforce to assume the jobs vacated by men. Thus their frivolous and time-killing activities were over. Many valentines still put together by hand disappeared in an age when such work was deemed quite unnecessary.

In addition, the war caused paper shortages. German items were no longer shipped to the United States and many Americans refused to purchase German items still in stock in American stores. Americans found it distasteful to purchase items made by a country with which they were at odds. World War I ended three English printers doing business with German printers: Davidson Brothers, the Artistic Lithographic Company, and W. Hagelberg. This affected the card market in a drastic manner in that much artistry and manufacturing skill was immediately lost as a result.

Davidson Brothers produced valentines of exquisite taste, using some very large elegant chromolithographs with inordinate detail. This decade was their strongest in production terms, having produced them in the early 1880s up to World War I. The Artistic Lithographic company, with its headquarters in Munich, also contributed thousands of different valentine designs, from the very small to the large foldouts with elaborate honeycomb and standing figures. W. Hagelberg, located in Berlin, was known for its mechanical cards incorporating hands and feet which moved. Eyes that opened and closed were also a favorite. Most of these cards also incorporated honeycomb as part of their design.

Fold-out ship, 12" X 10", marked "Germany." $140-160.

Fold-down cart, 12" X 10",
marked "Germany." $105-125.

Example of hold-to-light back with cellophane
behind letters, 6" X 10", Germany. $55-65

Honeycomb lighthouse, 8" X 10",
Raphael Tuck. $100-125.

Die-cut back with cellophane greetings, "Valentine Greeting", 6" X 8", Germany. $45-55.

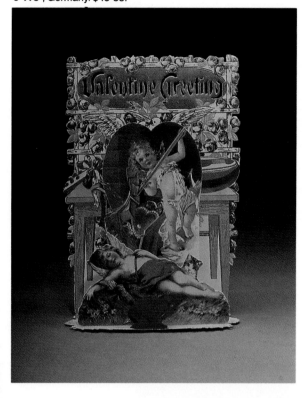

Fold-down carriage, 6" X 10", marked "Germany." $95-120.

Honeycomb gondola, 16" X 5", some damage due to missing pieces, Raphael Tuck. $35-45. *If perfect:* $150-175.

Simple pull-downs, 3 ½" X 5", Germany. $10-15 each.

Intricately detailed children on pull-downs, 4" X 6", Germany. $20-25 each.

Three elaborate examples of cellophane panes for hold-to-light effect, Germany. $40-50 each.

Simple fold-downs, wide-eyed girl is reminiscent of Chloe Preston's children. $10-15 each.

Simple 4" X 6" pull-downs, Germany. $20-30 each.

Pull-down with intricately embossed and die-cut cardboard back, 14" X 12", marked "Germany." $120-140.

One way to get a flavor for valentines of certain periods is to view catalog pages which illustrate such items for sale. March Brothers of Lebanon, Ohio, in their *1911 Holiday Requisites and Specialties* illustrate some of the valentines available that year. A glimpse of these catalog pages provides much insight into the types of valentines produced as well as typical prices for this decade.

Valentines.

IN VALENTINES we offer the very best goods obtainable anywhere. We have the cream of all lines, domestic and foreign. We give the biggest value for the money obtainable anywhere. Notice descriptions and prices below.

In many schools a delightful time is had by having a postoffice in the schoolroom. Allow the scholars to send valentines to one another (**not** comics). The teacher may send one to each scholar. This will create an era of good feeling.

Handsome Lace Valentines.

No. LV 1.

No. LV 1. Embossed flower designs in gilt and colors, with a variety of half-tone centers. Rococo edges, folding, appropriate verse inside. Very pretty. 4 x 5 inches, with envelope, 1 cent each

No. LV 2.

No. LV 2. Charming floral designs, in gilt and colors. Embossed Rococo edges, folding, artistic centers. Appropriate verse. Sure to please. 4¾ x 6½ inches, with envelope, 2 cents each.

No. LV 5.

No. LV 3. White lace and delicate ornaments springing from embossed backs in beautiful colors. Rococo edges, folding. Appropriate verse inside. A very dainty valentine. With envelope, 3 cents each.

No. LV 5. Richly embossed backs in gold and delicate colors. Exquisite new design in white lace, with a variety of choice ornaments. Appropriate verse. Rococo edges, folding, 6½ x 6½ inches. With envelope, 5 cents each.

Valentine Cards.

These cards are very delicate in color, pleasing in style and shape, and artistic in manufacture. Many prefer the cards to the more showy lace variety. We have the following:

No. VC 1. Various fanciful shapes, with delicately colored pictures of birds, flowers and little tots. Very pretty. 1 cent each.

No. VC 2. Very choice cards, a variety of shapes and pictures, all equally dainty and pleasing. Embossed, cut out shapes, very desirable. 2 cents each.

No. VC 3. An exceedingly artistic line of cut out shape cards, some folding, embossed, highly embellished. Very striking and beautiful. 3 cents each.

No. VC 5. Very elaborate folding cards, many novel shapes. Richly decorated. A fine style. 5 cents each.

No. VC 10. Similar to above, but larger and better. A variety of odd shapes and effects. Beautiful and pleasing. 10 cents each.

We have finer cards, any price you wish to pay. Order what you want, **and** we will guarantee that our selection will please you.

No. VD 1
and de
rious
beautif
tions w
each.

We ha
State price y
tion to suit.

No. VB 6.
Very pr
monotin

No. VB 1
colors a
open wo
colors.

Innumer
handsome st
ment, profuse
amatory miss

No. V
shaped
from to
sel supp

No. VI
shapes
The d
choice
15c. eac

No. V
shapes, l
of parc
celluloid
handsom
rated. 2

No. V
Unique s
styles, d
appropri
embellish
rich and t
each.

No. VD 10.

$1.00 Novelty.

Higher-Pric

We have a large and complete sto sizes, made of various materials, hand 60c, 75c, $1.00, $1.25, $1.50, $2.00, the amount you wish to pay, and w satisfaction. We issue a special ca trade. Dealers please send for it.

ne · Drops.

style valentine, very choice,
ing. Embossed cards in va-
licately colored, containing
spended in three or four sec-
on. For all ages. 10 cents

ps for those who want them.
ay and we will send a selec-

Booklets.

board, with rococo edges.
colors. Text illustrated in
nches. 6 cents each.

orate covers decorated in
ococo edges, some made of
nside illustrated in choicest
½ x 5 inches. 10 cents.

Novelties.

apes, fancy designs, and
silk, celluloid and parch-
ly decorated. Very choice
e in a box.

No. V N 10.

No. V N 15.

ties, of all shapes and
hly decorated, at 50c,
.oo and $5.00. Send
ection and guarantee
es for the wholesale

Valentine Specialties.

Choice High-Grade Valentine Post Cards.

A charming series of clever and artistic Post Cards, excellently colored, bearing appropriate messages. Sensible, nonsensical, or humorous. Nothing inelegant or offensive. **One cent each for any number over five.** A delightful series, as follows:

G407. Love's Playtime. Little folks. Very artistic and cunning. 1c each for 5 or more.

G404. Love's Messengers. Cupids, hearts and flowers. Very dainty. 1c. each for 5 or more.

G400. Affinities. Funny fruits and vegetables. Coupling hat pins, etc. 1c. each for 5 or more.

G1406. Love Missives. Comic children and comic sentiments. 1c. each for 5 or more.

G1402. Sweethearts True. High School Favorites. New and up-to-date. 1c. each for 5 or more.

T101. Love Bulletins. Merry faces and greetings. Humorous.

T8. Buster Brown. Funny pranks and sayings. 1c. each for 5 or more.

T1. Slates. Comic Kids. Comic comments. 1c. each for 5 or more.

G405. Merry Little Lovers. Children. Colonial, Scotch, Dutch, Indian. Up-to-date. 1c. each for 5 or more.

T100. Miscellaneous Comics. Musical Coons, Dutch Love songs, etc. 1c. each for 5 or more.

Valentine Letters.

Beautiful Valentine Missives in highly artistic letter form, appropriately decorated with cupids and flowers, conventional designs, etc., elegantly printed. Exquisite color effects. Folders, with envelopes, as follows:

G490. Flowers and Cupids. Sentimental messages. 3¾x5¾ in., 5 cents each.

G491. Humorous Children. Comical text, 3¾x5¾ in., 5 cents each.

G495. Sly Little Cupid. With dainty floral decoration. Very choice. 6¾x5 in., 10 cents each.

G498. Loving Missives. Die-stamped, richly illuminated and embossed text. Artistic and exquisite in detail. "Heart's Dearest," "My Valentine," etc., 6x8 in., 10 cents each.

G423. Night Letter. "Authentic." Direct from Dan Cupid's Telegraph Co., 7x8 in., 1 cent each for five or more.

New Idea Valentines.

VARIOUS UNIQUE SURPRISES IN VARIOUS UNIQUE FORMS.

G447. Komic Kids, Dainty Ladies, Hoodwinks, Love Hearts, etc., 5 cents each.

G449. Goo-Goo Eyes. Very droll children with "busy" (movable) eyes. 5 cents each.

G465. Sunbonnet Sue, Parasol Prue, etc., with movable sunbonnets and parasols. 10 cents each.

G443. Happy Hearts Blotters, Forget-Me-Not Fans, Busy Dan Cupid, etc., 5 cents each.

T600. Pulling Cards, "A." Children's Floral novelty. 3 cents each.

G478. Pulling Cards, "B." Large floral novelty. 5 cents each.

G473. Wireless Messages, Tie That Binds, Key to My Heart, Cupid's Quiver, Special Delivery, etc., 10 cents each.

G467. Love Provokers. Sweethearts and Scissors, Cat in the Bag, Just One Girl, etc., 10 cents each.

T45. Hidden Jokes, Comic Coons, Bad Bargains, Name the Day, 23Skidoo, etc., 10 cents each.

T80. Love Lessons. Will delight little folks. Very pleasing, bright and amusing. 15 cents each.

G488. My Heart's in My Mouth. Humorous, mechanical child with movable mouth. 15 cents each.

G489. Twirlers. Two-sided droll figures of children. On sticks. Movable arms and legs. 15 cents each.

T610. Dutch Pulling Card. Mechanical, artistic and comical. 15 cents each.

T614. Charming Colonial Figures. Very artistic. Mechanical. 20 cents each.

G479. Artistic Floral Pulling Card. Cupids, flowers, hearts, etc. 10 cents each.

Ordinary Comic Valentines.

We supply the ordinary Comic Valentines (paper 7½x10 inches), at 7 cents a dozen. In this style we have Sharp Dots, Don'ts, Hall of Fame, Ordinary Trades, etc. Buster Brown Comics, same size, but newer and more unique; 10 cents per dozen. Hit 'Em Hard, extra large size, 15 cents dozen.

One facet of Valentine's Day not yet covered is the envelopes in which the early cards were placed. Most of these envelopes were decorated, often delicately printed, and sometimes embossed. Unfortunately after having served their purpose, they were often thrown away. Often the envelopes were expressly produced for a particular valentine. But for those who could not afford this luxury, packets in varying sizes for general use were sold. At first little wafers were used to seal the envelopes as an alternative to wax. It was not until the mid 1850s that envelopes appeared with gummed flaps.

In this decade, elegantly embossed and lacy envelopes continued to contain very elegant valentines. Since Americans had perfected the art of lace making and had improved their methodology in paper manufacturing, these envelopes were more within the reach of the average person. Lace continued to be incorporated on many valentines of this period. In fact, this type of valentines was referred to as the "old-fashioned type" by many of the jobbers who sold these products to department stores and various mail order houses.

This continued to be an era of elegance as many Americans shunned the popular fold-outs, honeycombs, and comic valentines and continued to cling to the lacy, fold-over card. While some of these were still manufactured in Germany, England, and France; the majority of the lacy valentines found today by collectors were produced by George Whitney who had a large share of the American card market at this time. Whitney's cards have that distinctive classic look which he continued to follow in this period up to the start of World War I. Whitney's cards were priced in the retail market from one to fifty dollars, but the high end items declined in popularity.

George C. Whitney continued his active involvement in the business for up to two years before his death on April 1, 1915. His son Warren A. Whitney continued the family business until it was liquidated in 1942.

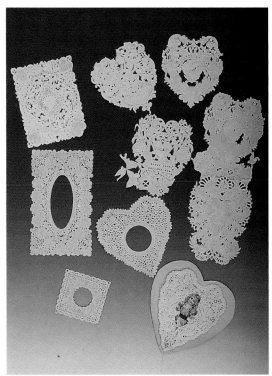

Sheets of lace produced in U.S. for manufacturers as well as home crafters. $2-7 each.

George Whitney manufactured cards, 1914. $10-15 each.

Early examples of American-produced embossed envelopes. $3-5 each.

Two old-fashioned cards, top with fine lace and bottom with fashionably dressed lady. *Top:* $20-25. *Bottom:* $25-30.

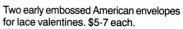

Two early embossed American envelopes for lace valentines. $5-7 each.

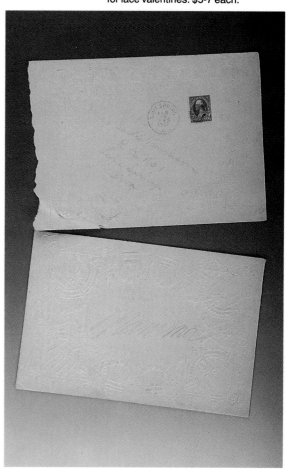

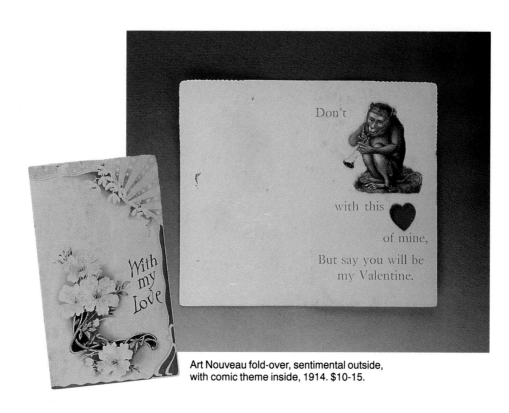

Art Nouveau fold-over, sentimental outside, with comic theme inside, 1914. $10-15.

Above: Old fashioned flower themed cards with sentimental verses inside each card. $5-7 each.

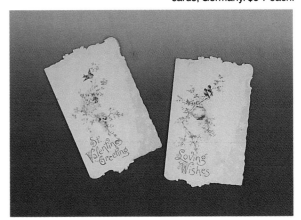

Below: Traditional tri-fold cards, Germany. $5-7 each.

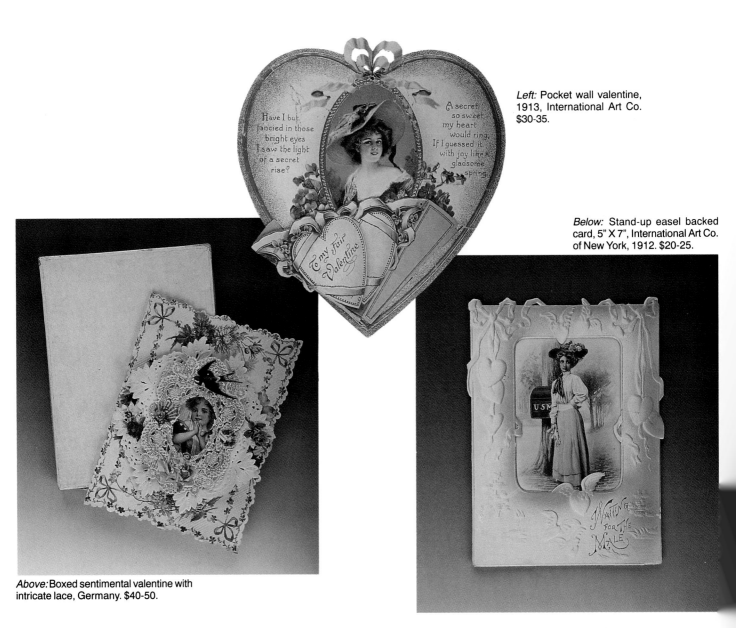

Left: Pocket wall valentine, 1913, International Art Co. $30-35.

Below: Stand-up easel backed card, 5" X 7", International Art Co. of New York, 1912. $20-25.

Above: Boxed sentimental valentine with intricate lace, Germany. $40-50.

Traditional flat valentines, all German. $2-3 each.

Left: Traditional flats with design on front and elegant sentimental verse on back. $2-4 each.

Heart-shaped fold-overs, all German. $2-5 each.

Above and Left: Traditional Ernest Nister designed valentines. $5-8 each.

Traditional Raphael Tuck designs. $3-5 each.

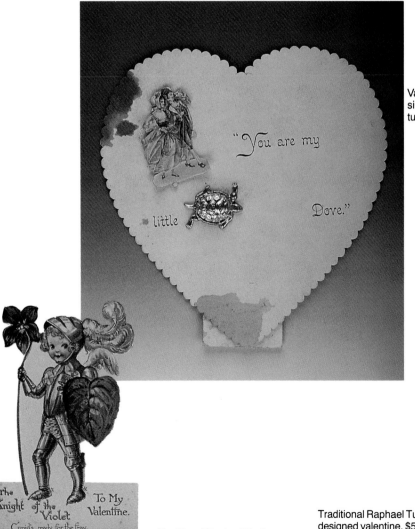

Valentine with chromolithograph, silk ribbons, and attached metal turtle token, 1914. $15-20.

Traditional Raphael Tuck designed valentine. $5-7.

Traditional Raphael Tuck designed valentine. $5-7.

This was a period when American cards started coming into their own. Valentine postcards really took on an American flavor when Stecher Lithograph Company of Rochester, New York, started manufacturing their own cards, many of which are marked "Made in U.S.A." While numerous valentine themed cards were created, those Stecher cards which contain children are the most distinctive. Some of the earliest Stecher children were Dutch, extremely popular between 1907 and 1915. Rosy-cheeked, red-lipped American kids with bright eyes that barely contain their mischief burst forth on most Stecher cards.

The earliest cards were embossed (up to the 700 series) with a few exceptions. However, with the advent of World War I, the demand for fancy postcards diminished, and like most printers, Stecher made mostly unembossed cards of an inferior quality. The most successful type of cards in their later years were the valentines meant to be sent to children. Hearts and flowers were a background for fuzzy animals and moon-faced little people. In later decades, these cards were sent more by children than by adults who considered it in poor taste to send a personal message on St. Valentine's Day for all to read. Therefore, the cards produced in subsequent years illustrate the custom of children sending valentines in the 1930s by using children as the main design theme. Unfortunately, most of the artists' whose illustrations were published by Stecher did not sign their name, so there is no way of attributing the art work. A certain number of later valentines were initialed "M.E.P."

Stecher cards are quite easy to identify. Many have "Stecher Lith Co. Roch, N. Y." around a small "Copyright C" on the face or on the picture side of the card. A few have a six-pointed star with the word "Stecher" on the upper left hand corner of the message side. Even when there is no trademark, the distinctive scroll on the back is easy to identify. Only the "C" in Card is ornamented with curlicues extending under the words "Post Card." The series number appears in the lower left hand corner in the message page.

Tuck, PFB, and other richly decorated and embossed cards. $5-10 each.

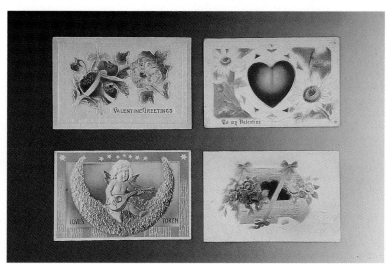

Above: Air-brushed postcard valentines, all deeply embossed. $5-7 each.

Right: More rare and desirable postcards, all German, with sentimental scenes. $7-12 each.

More rare postcards, all which incorporate a comic theme so popular earlier in the decade. $10-15 each.

Artist-signed sentimental postcards, Germany and United States. $10-20 each.

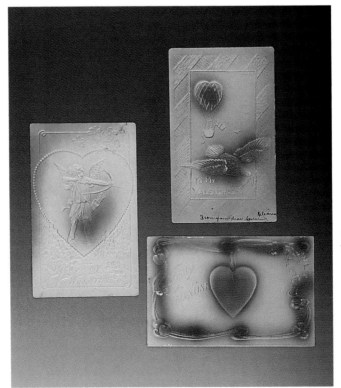

More common air-brushed valentine postcards. $3-5 each.

Tuck, Stecher, and Whitney postcards with heart-themed sentiments. $10-20 each.

Assortment of Stecher produced postcards. $5-15 each.

Dutch themed valentines, extremely popular up to World War I. $5-10 each.

Other American companies had their beginnings in this decade as well. One such company was Rust Craft of Boston. The company began when Fred Winslow Rust, whose hobby of collecting Prang prints and picture cards, inspired him to open a one-room book shop on the second floor of a Kansas City office building. Within one month of opening his business, he published a greeting card of his own. His first cards were marked with a red capital "C." In 1907, his brother Donald joined him and the response was so tremendous that they printed their first valentines in 1909. By 1910, the business had developed to the point that they closed their retail shop and divided duties. Fred handled the creation and sales while Don handled the manufacturing and financial details. In 1913, to be more near their supply sources, they moved to Boston and became "Rust Craft Publishers." It was in this year that "Rust Craft" was imprinted on their cards as an identifying label.

Another American company, the Gibson Art Company continued to produce their own cards. Gibson cards quickly became known for their quality valentines often marked with a blue or green "G" or merely "Gibson Greetings" used later in their manufacturing years.

An early creator of valentines was Paul Vollard of Chicago who started his business in the summer of 1908. A native of Germany, Vollard was a genius for recognizing beauty in design and was the first to used mottled and clouded effects on cardboard. Vollard also was among the first to utilize the new offset process on greeting cards. The artists he used for producing his creative cards included Janet Laura Scott, Ella Brison, Catherine Sturgis Dodge, Frederick Richardson, John Gruell, and John Roe. Unfortunately his career ended in

tragedy when a mentally ill woman shot him during a conference in his private office. The company was then led by F. J. Clampitt, a silent partner in the business since it had been founded.

Still another well-recognized company, "The Buzza Company" had its start in 1909 when a commercial artist, George Buzza drifted into the card business. With his combined talents of artistry, designing, engraving, and printing; he quickly established a lucrative firm. Around 1915, Alfred G. Anderson and H. B. Swartwood joined the company and took the firm past the one-man operation it had been. Artists such as Lee Mero, Bernice Shaver, and Janet Scott added much to the early company's success as well.

Many of these valentines were sold by various companies by means of a mail order catalog. David C. Cook Publishing Company of Elgin, Chicago, New York, and Boston advertised cards and party supplies in their 1917 catalog. The sparse war years were apparent from the selection of materials offered for sale. Valentine postcard invitations, celluloid pin-back buttons, and badges made of strong enameled paper were among those items advertised. For one cent each, there was a series of six rocking horse themed American-printed cards along with an assortment of holiday postcards sold at ten sets or more—100 cards for the price of $1.00. Heart-shaped German printed cards (still in stock no doubt as they were not available that year from Europe) sold for 1/2 cent each complete with envelopes. In these lean war years, very little was available.

Outside of fold card, very simple in style, inside of card revealed glued-on postcard and valentine verse on left inside fold. $15-20.

Chapter VII
New Designs Emerge:
1920-1929

The period immediately after World War I is important in valentine history. In the years after the war, Americans changed in so many ways. New prosperity, the emergence of the American female, and many other social trends definitely affected the customs of sending valentines as well as the designs manufactured. No longer seen as feeble and weak individuals, American women became hard-looking, hard-working flappers with flat chests and bobbed hair.

Although Americans enjoyed economic prosperity in the 1920s, Europe suffered some disastrous economic times. Many German lithographers closed their doors, some of whom were Littauer & Boysen (L & B), Zoecke & Mittmeyer, and Mamelok Press. In this decade, the craftsmanship to produce fine quality valentines had all but disappeared. While cards from the earlier part of this decade immediately after World War I continued to be like those before the war, changes were taking place. In the latter part of this decade

cards were much more simple in style and less cluttered. Thus Rose O'Neill's Kewpies, Grace Drayton's Dolly Dingles, and Berth Kammer's Sunbonnet Babies became immensely popular. Popular mechanical valentines now featured moving eyes, arms, legs, etc. rather than three-dimensional scenes.

But for many, the elegant fold-out valentines continued to be a favorite of those who clung to past traditions. Some individuals thought it extremely offensive to send "modern" cards. " 'Love never fades,' so why should we change?" was the chant of many card senders. For those who had more money and were willing to gamble this money on winning the love of a favored one, large elaborate cards incorporating honeycomb were available for the grand total of 49 cents for a card up to 12 inches in height. For those with in-between pockets, 29 cents was the going rate. And, of course, the one, two, and five cent variety continued to sell the best as these cards were well within the reach of most individuals.

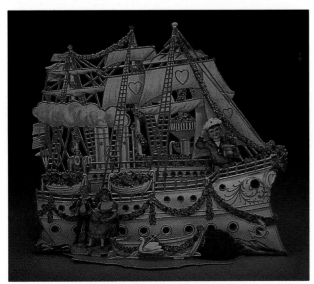
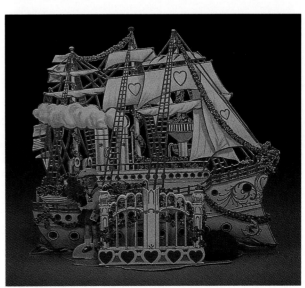

Large pull-down ship with intricate riggings, 14" X 12", advertised as set in 1922, Germany. $160-180.

Rare 14" X 16" fold-down airplane with angel inside, red crepe paper, cardboard wings, 1927. $260-285.

Victorian style carriage in front of beautifully detailed house, sold in box, 1923. $175-200.

Matching set of windmill fold-downs, 14" X 16," sold as set in 1926. $120-140 each.

Rare 14" X 16" fold-down airplane, honeycomb and crepe paper, cardboard wings, 1927. $250-275.

Large ship with rare honeycomb sail, 6" X 11", held in place by string which pulls from back, Germany. $95-115.

Sewing machine with girl, 6" X 8" honeycomb valentine from 1924, Germany. $75-85.

Fold-down in rare subject theme, four-leaf clover clock, 6" X 12", 1927, Germany. $55-65.

Elaborately chromolithographed children with parasol, 7" X 13", 1928, Germany. $40-50.

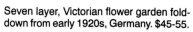
Seven layer, Victorian flower garden fold-down from early 1920s, Germany. $45-55.

Simple three layer, flower garden presented in1921, Germany. $30-40.

Angel in daisy flower cart, 15" X 8" fold-down, Germany 1922. $75-95.

Fold-downs, 4" X 9", 1927, Germany. $20-30.

Simple fold-down, 6" X 8", Germany. $25-35.

Sailing theme fold-down, 4" X 8", Germany. $30-35.

Sailor honeycomb valentine,
4" X 5", 1922. $30-40.

Set of nautical themed honeycombs,
1925. *Right:* $30-35. *Left:* $10-15.

Honeycomb valentine,
10" X 15", 1929. $35-45.

Three unusual honeycomb
valentines, early 1920s,
Germany. $40-50 each.

Both were sent to a little girl, Ethel, in 1927 in same envelope, Germany. $20-30 each.

Assortment of one cent valentines, Germany. $3-7 each.

One cent valentines, 1920s, all sent to one Missouri teacher, Germany. $3-5 each.

Assortment which sold for two cents each, Germany. $5-7 each.

Three simple small fold-downs, Germany. $5-15 each.

Valentines, 4" X 5", Germany. $5-10 each.

Simple pull-downs by Raphael Tuck. $10-12 each.

Simple paper lithographed fold-downs, 4" X 4" cards sent to Adelaide in 1921. $25-30 each.

Fold-out layered valentine, Germany. $20-25.

Variety of fold-outs, 1923, Germany. $10-15 each.

Although Art Deco had its roots in the previous decade, it was not until the 1920s that valentines reflected the popularity of this movement in 1925. *Art Deco* emerged as a reaction to *Art Nouveau*. Art Deco cards are recognized by their highly stylized natural and geometric forms and ornamentation, usually strongly symmetrical. Art Deco valentines were often classical motifs reduced to geometric stylizations. American manufactured valentines especially reflected this artistic trend.

Art Deco theme card, 2" X 4", open and closed view. $10-12

Variety of Art Deco cards, 2" X 4", American. $3-5 each.

One artist who gained much prominence in this decade was Charles R. Twelvetrees who designed for Alpha Publications, S. Bergman, Edward Gross, National Art Company, Reinthal & Newman, F.A. Stokes, Raphael Tuck, and Ullman Manufacturing Company. One of his characteristics is chubby children with fat, plump faces with witty and humorous verses for valentines starting in the 1920s and continuing through the 1930s. Very little is known of his life. History records his death on April 7, 1948 in the Hotel Le Marquis in New York, New York.

Twelvetrees signed postcard valentines, 1920s. $5-10 each.

Art Deco style booklets with inserts, 1923. $5-10 each.

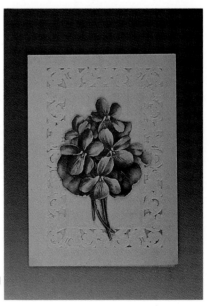

Card with simple violet spray on outside and Art Deco theme inside, 4" X 5". $7-10.

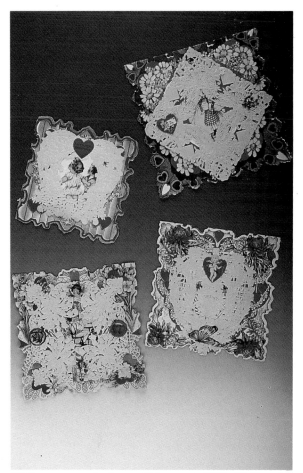

Whitney square valentines, with lace, early 1920s. $5-10 each.

Warren W. Whitney continued his father's business in the 1920s. The company was down to about 300 employees in a decade when there was intense competition in valentines production. Whitney had offices located in Boston, New York, and Chicago. In this decade, the most expensive valentine retailed by Whitney was five dollars, a real change from previous times. More and more cards were sold in sets for school children, thus the need for larger more elaborate cards somewhat declined. In fact it was the custom of exchanging valentines in school which was very instrumental in keeping alive card traditions. Children always brought a valentine to their teacher, and in this way many a school teacher's popularity was waged. Pupils brought their valentines to be placed in a box, and then were given out as part of a Valentine's Day party. Other companies such as Hallmark, Buzza, and Rust Craft had taken a large portion of the large card market away from Whitney.

Whitney heart cards, mid-1920s. $10-12 each.

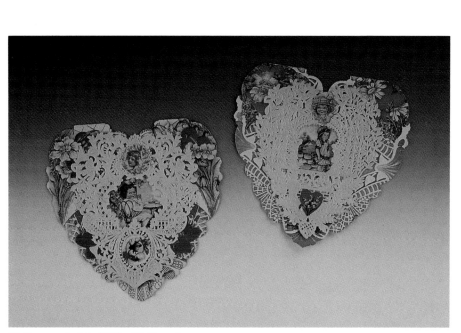

Whitney cards, late 1920s. $5-10 each.

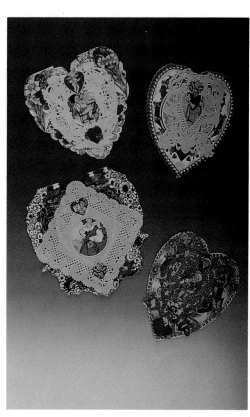

Right: Four heart-shaped Whitney valentines, 2-5 cents each for original price. $12-15 each.

Left: Five rectangular-shaped Whitney valentines, higher end cards. $20-25 each.

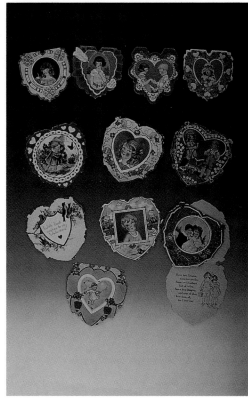

Variety of simple Whitney valentines, inexpensive assortment. $2-7 each.

Whitney cards, mid-1920s. $5-10 each.

Assorted inexpensive Whitney cards meant for exchanging at school. $2-5 each.

Assortment of inexpensive heart-shaped Whitney cards for school exchanging. $3-6 each.

Assortment of inexpensive Whitney cards meant for exchanging at school. $3-5 each.

The production techniques for scraps used in German-manufactured designs changed due to inferior, mass-produced scraps printed from photographic plates and restrictions imposed by World War I. Poor quality paper which caused the inks to "bleed" produced inferior scrap. More inexpensive materials were used after the war and the economic recession of the 1920s took its toll. Raphael Tuck was successful in reviving the valentines marketed during this decade, thus ensuring some artistic quality and a continuance of the fold-down valentines, even if they were far less elaborate. Graphics were more linear, more abstract. Colors became very exotic, reflecting the 1920s artistic movements. Everything became less cluttered.

Fold-out book types, American. $2-5 each.

American manufactured valentines, 3" X 4". $2-3 each.

Sunbonnet card, 1920s. $10-15.

Below: Simple American postcard valentines, 1920s. $3-7 each.

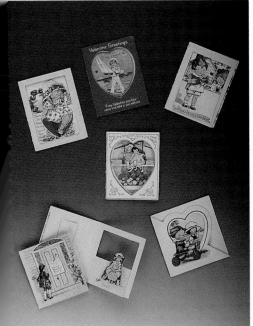

Above: American postcards reflecting simple designs. $1-3 each.

Left: Simple small 2" X 3" American made cards. $1-3 each.

World War I prompted a great increase in greeting card popularity, directly resulting in success for many American companies, including Gibson. Since many other companies entered the market and competed for a portion of the valentine sales, Gibson refined its printing process, art techniques, and decorative finishing techniques. Gibson is credited with popularizing the "French Fold" card—one sheet of paper folded in half twice—which became a best-selling greeting card form and an industry standard.

Replacing many of the German manufactured valentines were those tissue-paper honeycomb valentines manufactured in the United States. Beistle of Shippensburg, Pennsylvania had produced various types of meshed tissue over the years. However, their entry into the valentine's greeting card business began in 1925.

Beistle was founded in Pittsburgh by Martin Luther Beistle who worked for a calendar company, selling calendars to businesses in the area. While making his rounds, he became intrigued with the concept of producing artificial ferns and palms like the ones he saw in various hotel lobbies. His wife Anna Mary, their housekeeper, and he started a business producing decorative objects. Enjoying great success, he then purchased his employer's calendar business. Fifteen patents were taken out, starting in 1904. Five of these were for meshed-tissue items in which Beistle would come to specialize: baskets, garlands, and ornaments with scraps. Economic panic in 1907 forced this young firm to consolidate and return to Shippensburg. In 1909, a catalog of theirs offered tissue paper valentines from Germany.

It was in the mid 1920s that Beistle entered the card market. The company designed, produced, and marketed valentines from 1925 until the start of World War II. During this period over a thousand different valentines were manufactured, with over 425 of them incorporating meshed tissue. Beistle cards closely resembled the German cards of this period, but their heavier cardboard stock and printing designed by American artists soon created a new distinctive appearance.

Their first valentines, traditional pulldowns, of which 110 different examples were produced, became almost immediately successful. All have a disc of honeycomb called a "rosette" placed on the inside of the card's flap or base. German valentines used these rosettes to hide the glued hinges for the card's standup parts. For Beistle they were simply colorful decorative elements. Some cards had scraps inserted in the tissue rosette; others had embossed as well as printed designs of the card's top face, and they often had easel backs. The verse was usually printed on the underside of the flap.

Above: Beistle valentine incorporating honeycomb in upper part of valentine—German chromo with rest of card printed in United States. $20-30.

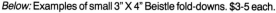

Below: Examples of small 3" X 4" Beistle fold-downs. $3-5 each.

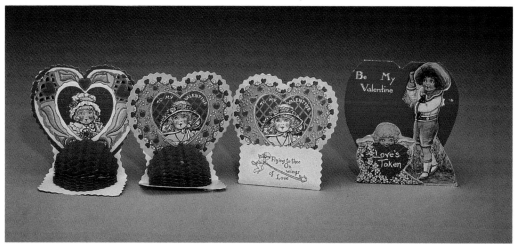

Late 1920s Beistle valentines in 3" to 4" styles. $3-5 each.

Variety of styles produced by Beistle incorporating honeycomb canopies and popular fold-out style. $5-10 each.

One very distinguishing and creative example of valentines produced by Beistle were those termed "canopies." Canopy cards had large, complex honeycomb parts that dominated the entire valentine. These more expensive cards at first resembled fountains or lamps and played off art work suggestive of these items. In 1929 such cards wholesaled for 200 dollars a thousand. Seventy-seven different designs have been documented. There are three distinct parts: a base, a pedestal, and a top. Usually red tissue was used for all three elements, but rarer examples used three distinctly different colors: deep blue, magenta, and red. Twenty-nine other examples were manufactured which contained only the top and the bottom, eliminating the pedestal.

Some canopy cards were in the shapes of baskets,as large as 10". As with some of the canopies, the cards were opened fully—in the round. Their handles, of sturdy cardboard, were printed on both sides with colorful red and white decorative hearts. Some of these cards had honeycomb shapes that snapped into place within the baskets. Produced as early as 1929, they continued in production into 1937.

Large 11" X 13" Beistle with blue flower panels on side. $35-45.

Mid-size 9" Beistle with smallest 4" canopy style produced by Beistle. *Left:* $35-40. *Right:* $5-10.

Left: One of the first Beistle double color canopy styles, 7" X 9." $20-25.

Above: Two large Beistle valentines with rare two-color style on left. *Left:* $20-25. *Right:* $25-30.

Left: Two more elaborate 11" Beistle style valentines. $25-35 each.

Above: Little girl in 6" Beistle basket in most simple style produced. $30-40.

Above: Two small late 1920s Beistle with more desirable lithographed one on right. $5-12 each.

Below: One of the first Beistle basket styles produced in 1929 with honeycomb hearts which are inserted in fold-out basket. $45-55.

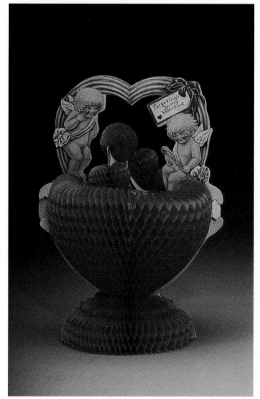

Beistle 12" basket with honeycomb heart inserts, one of their most popular style baskets. $45-55.

Mechanical Valentines
Intrigue and Attract Interest

Although the idea for mechanical valentines, pull tabs, rivets, and folding paper were in use in previous decades; it was not until the 1920s that mechanical valentines were produced by the thousands. Part of the reason lay in the fact that fold-out valentines and simple folder-type cards just did not attract the number of buyers as in previous times. Therefore, card manufacturers needed a gimmick to attract a newer and younger clientele. Mechanical cards intrigued the very young with their animation in a time when moving pictures started talking and Americans went to the movies every week.

Mechanical valentines were manufactured in both Germany and the United States. The European cards were more expensive and tended to be larger in size as well as more artistically designed. German cards usually incorporated more than two moving parts as well. German mechanical valentines dominated the scene just after World War I. By the end of the decade, American card manufacturers, seeing the market potential of such cards, quickly imitated the German ones and started flooding the market with more inexpensive, and in some cases, even more creative cards.

German 7" X 12" mechanical with moving orchestra and dancers on left—one of the more elaborate mechanicals produced in this decade. $45-50.

German 4" X 6" mechanicals. *Left:* has eyes which change with wheel, *Right:* reveals two letter choice on girl's lap. $20-25 each.

German 10" X 12" mechanical with moving children in front row and teacher's pointing finger. $20-30.

Left: Dug-out baseball German mechanical with fold-out bleachers. $20-25.

German 12" X 8" mechanical with moving teeter-totter. $20-25.

German 5" X 7" mechanical with boy's foot moving to kick football. $5-10.

Variety of German mechanicals which all incorporate moving eyes with black themes. $20-45.

Variety of German mechanicals which were
sold in sets for school exchanging. $1-3 each.

Two large 8" X 11" German mechanicals
with moving eyes and hands. $5-7 each.

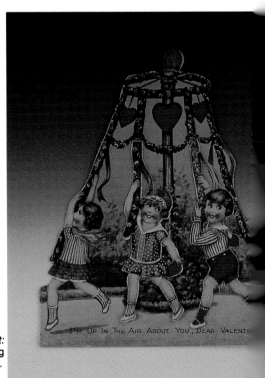

German 7" X 8" mechanicals. *Left:*
moving May pole children, *Right:* moving
merry-go-round children. $15-20 each.

Small 2" X 4" German mechanical cards which revealed children inside cars. $3-5 each.

Variety of more desirable German mechanicals including frog with four moving jointed legs. $20-25 each.

Large 5 cent German mechanical with 2 cent variety on right with moving periscope and arm. *Left:* $12-15. *Right:* $5-7.

Three musical mechanical valentines. *Left:* German-made.
Right: American-made. $3-5 each.

Rare style German mechanical valentines with
moving slits revealing hidden messages. $5-7 each.

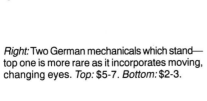

Above: Large 7" X 8" German mechanical
with moving fan in girl's hand. $7-10.

Right: Two German mechanicals which stand—
top one is more rare as it incorporates moving,
changing eyes. *Top:* $5-7. *Bottom:* $2-3.

116

American-made airplane mechanicals,
5" X 8". $10-15 each.

German-printed mechanical
fold-out, 5" X 8". $10-15.

American-printed mechanical fold-out with
German chromos, 5" X 7". $10-15 each.

Hallmark Makes Its Debut

Another American company, Hallmark cards, gained fame in this decade. Its history began on January 10, 1910, when a teenager from Norfolk, Nebraska, Joyce Hall arrived at the Kansas City train station. He had very little money—not even enough to take a horse-drawn cab to his lodgings at the YMCA—but he had some grand plans. Inside one of his bags were two shoe boxes full of picture postcards, and inside his head was a mail order plan for their distribution. Storing the inventory under his bed, Joyce Hall printed some invoices and started sending packets of a hundred cards to dealers in the Midwest. A few of the dealers kept the cards without paying and some returned the unsolicited merchandise with an angry note. But about a third of his customers sent a check, and within a few months, Hall had cleared two hundred dollars and opened a checking account.

Despite his success, Hall felt that postcards were a passing fancy and they would soon be out of vogue. He saw more of a market for higher quality valentines—mailed in envelopes. In 1912, a year after his brother Rollie joined him, Joyce Hall added greeting cards to the line. Their Hall Brothers store was destroyed in a 1915 fire just before Valentine's Day. But the Halls obtained a loan, bought an engraving company, and produced their own original cards in time for the Christmas season. Prosperity followed, and by 1922, after World War I, The Hall Brothers firm which now included a third brother, William F. Hall, employed 120 persons. They had salesmen in all 48 states and had begun offering gift wrap. At this point they started stamping the backs of their cards with "A Hallmark Card." In 1923, the company moved into its own six-story plant at 26th and Walnut, a site chosen by ballot among employees. Thus this decade found the first Hallmark cards for sale on Valentine's Day. By this time, the inventory had grown to 120 different cards, far above the four cards from the company's very humble beginnings.

Right: Assortment of cards in style of Hallmark used in 1920s. $5-7 each.

Below: Early Hallmark card with trademark on back. $10-15.

Right: Trio of 1920s cards attributed to Hallmark due to style and theme. $12-15 each.

Variety of home-crafted cards from older materials. $1-5 each.

Variety of home-crafted cards made in 1926. $2-5 each.

American Manufacturers Create Valentine Kits

One popular custom began in this decade. As early as 1915, Whitney pioneered a valentine-making kit. School children who wished to save some money, use some ingenuity, and keep busy after school now could create their own valentines with the kits provided. They only needed to supply scissors and glue. These kits became very popular, especially during the war years when mothers attempted to find projects for nighttime hours.

In the 1920s, Whitney continued to provide kits for those who wish to make their own valentines, but they included more scraps, lace, and even crayons with the paper and items for assembling the cards. The Gibson Company, Milton Bradley, and Whitman Publishing Company also produced such boxes of materials for assembling valentines. Some appeared in book form to be cut and assembled and included the envelopes for mailing them. This trend sparked the idea for many children to produce their own cards from magazine pictures and materials found around the home as had been done in simpler times. Therefore, many collections of valentines uncovered from this decade contain quite a few home-made varieties.

119

Front view of home crafted valentine's box made in 1923 from older materials. $35-40.

While the early 1920s were prosperous, 1929 brought the stock market crash with many adults being in bad financial shape. Card manufacturers, now more than ever, were forced to attract buyers. Mechanical valentines, which afforded a chance for whimsical diversion and a little creative humor, really became popular during this time. In David C. Cook's 1928 *Annual Catalog of Sunday School Supplies and Holiday Specialties*, it is interesting to review their selection of Valentine Day supplies to get a flavor for prices and availability of different styles in the late 1920s.

Valentine Day Supplies

4c **7593-J. Merry St. Valentine's Day.**—A unique entertainment filled with heart-shine and smile-shine. All music for songs given as well as words. **4 cts.**, postpaid.

INVITATION CARDS.

65 cts. 100 **1630-K. Valentine Day Invitation Post Card.**—Engraved card in colors, for school celebration. To send to absent members, parents and friends where the school has special exercises on this day. **65 cts. per 100**, postpaid.

1707-K. Valentine Party Invitation Post Card.—Engraved card, with evening invitation, **65 cts. per 100**, postpaid.

75 cts. 100 **515-K. Heart Sunday Invitation.**—Pretty card in shape of a heart, with announcement that next Sunday is Heart Sunday, with special exercises, and invitation to be present. Ten or more, **75 cts. per 100**, postpaid.

523-K. Sweetheart Party Invitation.—For Cradle Roll. Red, heart-shaped card. Attractive invitation to mother and baby to Valentine party. Size, 3½ x 3½. Ten or more, **75 cts. per 100**, postpaid.

BANGLES, BADGES AND PINS.

1½c **Valentine Day Bangles.**—For souvenirs Cut from sheet celluloid with stick-pin fastening. Engraved design in colors. Very pleasing. Size, 1¼ x ¾. Ten or more, **1½ cts. each.** Samples free.

3307-X.—Valentine Heart Design.

1¼c **3133-X. Valentine Day Pin.**—Celluloid finish button pins for Valentine Day souvenirs. Circle of hearts in red. Ground of pin in white, with band of gray. Ten or more, **1¼ cts. each**, postpaid.

20c **6897-Y. Valentine Day Flag.**—Flag especially for this occasion. White ground with red heart, above which are words "St. Valentine." For room decorations, processionals, etc. Extra large. Size, 12 x 18 inches. Mounted on sticks. Six or more, **20 cts. each**, postpaid. Sample, **25 cts.**

PLACE CARDS.

4267-X. Valentine Day Hearts.—Red cardboard-shaped hearts to be decorated for homemade valentines, invitations, menu cards, place cards, etc. Also for table decorations. Size, 3 x 3 inches. Package of 25 for **10 cts.**, postpaid. Three packages for **25 cts.**

4268-X. Valentine Day Arrows.—White cardboard-shaped arrows, 5 inches long. Package of 25 for **15 cts.**, postpaid. Three packages for **35 cts.**

4266-X. Valentine Day Cupid.—White cupid, 4 inches high, standing on red heart. **Price, 4 cts. each**, postpaid.

514-K. Jesus' Valentine.—Heart-shaped card with suitable verse, to be given children on Valentine Sunday, or at Valentine Party. Ten or more, **75 cts. per 100**, postpaid.

HONEYCOMB VALENTINE.

5c **3956-X.**—For 1928 we are listing this new honeycomb tissue stand-up. Opened, it stands 5½ inches high, with honeycomb column appearance on lace effect valentine. A striking novelty. **Price**, singly, **6 cts. each**; three or more, **5 cts. each**, postpaid.

VALENTINES.

¾c **649-K. Cupid Cut-Out Greeting Cards.**—Heart cut-outs, elaborated with cupids seated on doves delivering valentines. Colors bright and greetings appropriate. A pleasing novelty. Size, 3¼ x 3¼. 6 designs. **Price, ¾ cent each**, postpaid.

STAND-UP VALENTINE.

1c **677-K.—Cut-out, Stand-up Valentine Greeting Card.**—In bright colors and stands up. Shows children in act of presenting valentines. A pleasing novelty. Six designs. Size, 2⅝ x 4¾. **Price, 1 cent each**, postpaid.

¾c **650-K. Heart Cut-Out Card.**—A most attractive heart cut-out card, made to stand up by bending base back. Valentine greetings on each, with embossed pictures of children presenting valentines and flowers. Six designs, sent assorted. Size, 3 x 3. **Price, ¾ cent each, postpaid.**

NOVELTY HIGH BACK STAND-UP.

1c **647-K.**—A pleasing stand-up folder card, bound to win favor. Each depicts children at play or at rest, with suitable Valentine greeting in gold. Six styles. Average size, 2¾ x 4½. **Price, 1 cent each**, postpaid.

BLACKBOARD GREETING CARD.

3c **654-K**—A most pleasing novelty. By turning wheel, girl or boy seemingly writes valentine greeting on blackboard, then erases it. Pretty colors, size, 3 x 4. Two designs, assorted, each with glassine envelope. **Price, 3 cts. each**, postpaid.

1½c **651-K. Bird and Heart Series.**—Eleven designs of cut-out stand-ups, embossed and printed in bright colors. Decorated in hearts and flowers. Size, open, 4½ x 3¼ **Price, 1½ cts. each**, postpaid.

2c **516-K.—Attractive double cut-out card.** Engraved design in colors. Boy Scout with Valentine Flag, saluting sweetheart who occupies snow fort. Pleasing alike to young and old. Size (closed), 3½ x 3¾. Each card put up in separate white envelope. **Price, 2 cts. each**, postpaid.

4c **7378-J. Valentine Day Suggestions.**—Booklet of suggestions telling how to make the most of Valentine Day in the interest of the school, department and class. **4 cts.**, postpaid.

PROGRAM BLANKS.

75 cts. 100 **3930-X. Valentine Day Program Blank.**—Design of hearts, ribbon and conventional fleur-de-lis at top of first page. Engraved and embossed. Beautifully printed in colors. Balance of first page and all of pages 2, 3, and 4 blank for printed or written program. On heavy enamel paper. Size, 5¾ x 4¼. Ten or more, **75 cts. per 100**, postpaid.

VALENTINE DAY POST CARDS.

1c **1883-K. Heart Candy Box Post Card.**—A real novelty post card, which will more than please the recipient. Depicts a heart-shape box of candy, opened, with appropriate decorations. Greeting in colors, tinted stock. Four designs. **Price, 1 cent each**, postpaid.

1c **1884-K. Children's Valentine Wreath Series.**—A fine series of four cards with paneled effect and printed in dainty colors on fine white cardboard. An appropriate greeting on each. **Price, 1 cent each**, postpaid.

65 cts. 100 **1885-K. Valentine Day Cradle Roll Greeting Post Card.**—For Cradle Roll Superintendent to send to babies on Valentine Day. Attractive card with pleasing message. Engraved and printed colors. Ten or more, **65 cts. per 100**, postpaid.

12 cts. roll **6457-O. Valentine Day Crêpe Paper Strips.**—For room decoration. White crêpe paper with red hearts. Strips 2¼ inches wide. Rolls of 40 feet. **12 cts.**, postpaid.

CREPE PAPER.

6467-O. Valentine Day Hearts and Horseshoe.—Decorated crêpe paper in red, green, brown and pink, with gold trimmings. Rolls, 20 inches wide by 10 feet long, **18 cts. per roll**, postpaid. Ten or more rolls, **15 cts. each**, postpaid.

PAPER NAPKINS.

6486-O. Crêpe Paper Napkins.—For Valentine Day party. Effectively decorated with cupids and hearts. Beautifully printed in blue, red, and gold. **Price**, ten or more, **45 cts. per 100**, postpaid.

VALENTINE DAY SOUVENIR HEARTS.

1c **652-K. Red Cardboard Heart.**—Two inches long, with Valentine Day Greeting in white. Cord and tassel for attaching to clothing. Intended to be given out as souvenirs at Sunday-school on Valentine Day, or at entertainment. Ten or more, **1 cent each**, postpaid.

4400-X. Valentine Day Samples.—Contains two styles Invitation Post Cards, Bangle, Badges, Pin, Program Blanks, and Booklet of suggestions, **7 cts.**, postpaid.

Chapter VIII
The Advent of American Greetings:
1930-1939

This decade witnessed the revitalization of the valentine market through the practice of children exchanging valentines in school. While the sending of valentines among adults dwindled, children brought valentines to exchange with classmates and to give to their teachers. These valentines were made either by drawing them or by assembling them from published cards (saved from previous years), paper lace, and cut-outs (some provided by companies and some gleaned from colored pictures in magazines at home).

Most cards sold in the 1930s contained the words "Made in U.S.A." on the back of the cards with relatively few of them being identified by particular manufacturers. Most cards sold for one cent to five cents, with the most expensive cards being 10 cents. These prices attracted the young buyers who could not afford too much more, especially if they were to purchase valentines for all their classmates. The Carrington Company of Chicago, Illinois provided many mechanical cards containing tiny rivets which mechanized the card. One of their popular themes was black children. The Carrington Company bought out Whitney in 1942 and brought into its line many of Whitney's designs and patterns used on valentines. Carrrington went out of business in 1955.

Variety of American police themed cards all marked "Made in U.S.A." $2-5 each.

Carrington marked cards. *Left:* mechanical revealing couple in back. *Right:* stand-up. $10-15 each.

Two 5" X 6" American mechanicals with moving slits changing facial expressions. $3-5 each.

Two 4" X 5" American mechanicals with moving arms. $2-3 each.

An assortment from school child illustrating U.S.A. valentines, all marked 1932 on back by student. $2-5 each.

Two large 10" X 12" Art Deco themed mechanical American-made valentines. $5-10 each.

Two American mechanicals. *Left:* with protruding tongue. *Right:* with moving eyes and hands. $2-5 each.

Trio of American fold-over cards with verses inside. $1-3 each.

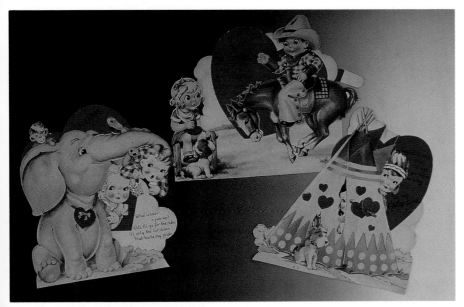

Trio of large 9" X 12" American mechanicals all marked 1934 on backs. $2-5 each.

Two very typical American cards revealing clothing fashions of the 1930s. $2-5 each.

A teacher's assortment of carefully labeled valentines (on each back) with the year that she received these cards from her students can reveal much history. A variety of cards from 1937 revealed social trends including movie making, fortune-telling machines, ladies dressed for the opera with lunettes, and students creating valentines from tissue hearts. Especially popular that year were mechanicals with rivets which produced swinging arms and changing eyes as well as a pussy cat in an apron pulling a gold fish from the fish bowl. Labels on the back included "Printed in Germany," "MADE IN U.S.A.," "RUST CRAFT BOSTON U.S.A.," "CARRINGTON" with a potted tree inside of which is a capital "E," and " A.C. Co. product of U.S.A."

American mechanical valentines from 1937, all between 5" X 7." $2-6 each.

Large 5" X 8" American mechanicals, 1937. *Left:* mechanical turning wheel on top. *Right:* swings back and forth, both with easel backs. $10-15 each.

American 4" X 6" mechanicals, 1937, with child in each airplane (sold as set). $5-10 each.

124

Variety of American
mechanicals. $10-15
each.

Medium sized American
valentines, all of which reveal
hidden message. $3-5 each.

Right: Large 6" X 8"
American mechanicals
with exact printing on
heavier cardboard stock.
$5-7 each.

Far right: Large detailed
American mechanicals
exchanged in 1935 at
"Prairie View School." $3-
6 each.

American-made black 5" X 6" mechanical which reveals slip when umbrella is raised. $15-20.

American 6" X 7" mechanical with moving wings. $2-5.

American 5" X 6" mechanical with moving hands and bear in back of igloo. $10-12.

Two cowboy related 1930s valentines reflecting children's fascination with cowboys and Indians. $3-5 each.

Variety of late 1930s valentines, most all of which are animal-themed. $2-3 each.

Variety of smaller inexpensive American-printed mechanicals, all sold in packages for school exchange. $1-2 each.

Variety of late 1930s valentines, all of which are mechanical and have attachments such as feathers and fake coins. $3-7 each.

Variety of simple flats which reveal simplistic Art Deco style still popular with adults. $1-3 each.

Variety of simple flats revealing various styles available in 1938 from American card makers. $1-2 each.

Assortment of fold-over cards popular towards end of 1930s. $1-2 each.

Assortment of food and flower related fold-over cards made in U.S.A. $1-2 each.

Food related fold-over cards exchanged in 1936 in rural Illinois school. $2-3 each.

Transportation was important to Americans in this decade and this is reflected in the modes of transportation as illustrated on valentines. Trucks, roadsters, buses, race cars, motorcycles, trains, pedal cars, planes, and zeppelins contained smiling children and fashionable adults carrying sentiments of love to someone they held close. From examining thousands of cards from this decade, it appears that the majority of transportation cards were produced by American printers.

One of these companies was Rust Craft who continued to produce countless valentines for the American market. As early as 1924, the Campbell Art Company's resources became a part of Rust Craft. In the 1930s, Rust Craft grew by leaps and bounds. Many of their children were drawn by Marion Justice, Betty Manley, Ruth Norton, and Gunila Stierngranat.

Fold-over cards all produced by "Rust Craft" of Boston. $2-5 each

Buzza continued to be a leader in the valentine business in this decade. Buzza's greatest coup (a decade earlier) was in 1922, when George Buzza convinced Edgar Guest to grant Buzza exclusive rights to the use of his writings in greeting cards and mottoes. This "Just folks" poet did much to advance the quality of Buzza's valentines. In the late 1930s, Buzza moved to Hollywood, California and was renamed "Buzza-Cardoza." From there the company progressed steadily. Another name, "The Norcross Company" had its start in 1914, but it wasn't until after World War I that this company came into its own under the direction of Arthur D. and Jane Norcross, brother and sister. Their early copper plate etchings, dry points, and engravings on hand-made papers, each hand-colored with envelopes to match produced some fantastic valentines. Their early 1920s color schemes required l2 to 35 different colors.

With mechanical valentines commercially produced, many teachers copied the idea and used this novelty in the classroom with their students to produce home-crafted valentines. In the January, 1932 January issue of *School Arts*, Flora V.

Shoemaker provides patterns which the body was traced onto drawing paper, colored with crayons and hearts were cut from red construction paper. The foot was made from black paper and fastened onto the heart with a small patent fastener. Some children wanted the valentine to stand so they pasted a half-inch strip of heavy drawing paper on back of the body part.

In this same issue Philomene Crooks presented an attractive variation from the usual valentine. She suggested that children make sachet nosegays for their parents, the flowers of which were made by cutting five petals from pastel shades of crepe paper. The extreme ends of the petals were then twisted slightly and one end of a piece of picture wire was bound around as to form a flower. These wires were in varying lengths and covered with thin bands of green crepe paper to form stems. A small envelope of sachet powder was next placed between the stems. The bouquet was placed in the center of a six-inch paper doily which was wrapped around it, and the entire valentine was finished with a silk ribbon tied around the nosegay.

In this decade Beistle produced valentines with very large rosettes which covered nearly all of the flap. A extremely large group of stand-up valentines with easel bases and substantial honeycomb bases which formed a deep semicircle when opened, were manufactured. Their art work was imprinted on the flat die-cut, sometimes embossed on heart-shaped backs. Over 172 different designs of this type were produced between 1929 and 1939. Seventeen of them incorporated meshed-tissue hearts on the card stock along with the tissue bases. "Photo prints," a photo-lithograph was used quite often as a part of the valentine. Some of the stand-ups had mechanical parts that were eyeleted such as tilting hats, rolling eyes, moving arms and legs, and even words that appeared or disappeared on a blackboard, for example. Large honeycomb hearts started to be produced in this decade, but it wasn't until the 1950s that their popularity abounded.

One other popular type manufactured by Beistle were novelties with honeycomb that appeared in forms other than hearts. Colonial dames with fully rounded honeycomb skirts, honeycomb wheels of motorcycles, and honeycomb umbrellas appeared in over 30 different novelties in the 1930s. Their last year of producing cards was 1939. At that time Beistle started producing the first in a series of giant honeycomb hearts, the largest of which was 27 inches. After World War II, Beistle produced primarily valentine centerpieces (1950s), hanging decorations (1960s), and garlands (1990s).

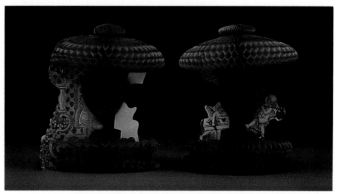

Popular 360-degree canopy Beistle valentines. $15-20 each.

Above: Large Beistle Colonial Dame
with honeycomb skirt. $40-50.

Below: Late 1930s Beistle with
honeycomb canopy. $25-30.

Large honeycomb heart produced over a long period of time by Beistle. $15-20.

Large 10" X 12" Beistle with insert arrow darts with verses on red string. $20-30.

Below: Style produced by Beistle, 1930s, with many attachments to honeycomb. $25-30.

Above: Large 9" X 11" Beistle canopy with 360-degree honeycomb also marketed as table centerpiece. $30-35.

This decade is of particular importance in that the four-color printing process which reduced all colors to four basics became standardized. Thus any color could be printed from a combination of these four. Finally, the need for laying the drawings for separate colors on steel plates or stones was eliminated. Consequently the cost of chromolithography, especially when compared to four-color printing, became prohibitive in price.

With Hitler's rise to power in Germany, many German lithographic companies were confiscated because their owners were Jews. Those who were able to flee had to leave many of their plates and archives behind. The Blitz reduced many factories to rubble.

One of the most tragic loss of the decade was the total destruction of Raphael Tuck's London headquarters on December 29, 1940. Subsequently rebuilt, this very famous company no longer had any record of its pre-1940 production.

When Allied bombers leveled German cities in retaliation, many German firms were lost forever. The partition of East and West Germany and the Communist takeover of Poland also destroyed much early history.

Some very excellent fold cards, flats, fold-downs, honeycombs, and mechanical valentines manufactured in Germany continued to be marketed in the United States until 1939 when the British Blockade prevented any European goods from being imported into the country. These goods were desirable because often times they could be brought in at less than Americans could produce for themselves. Pull-down valentines continued to attract those who had a little extra to spend and wished to impress the person for whom the card was intended.

Large 8" X 6" German pull-down with open lace back. $20-25.

German pull-down, 5" X 7", printed or unusually thick cardboard stock. $25-30

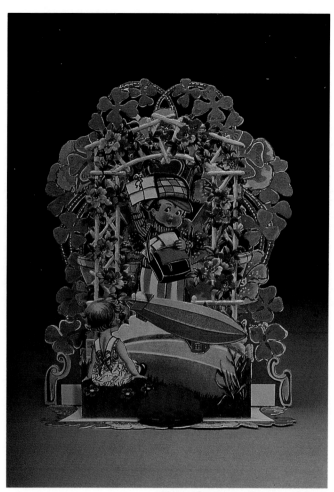

Above: German pull-down, 6" X 8", marked "1936" on back. $20-25 each.

Left: Early 1930s 5" X 9" German pull-down with elaborate flower detail still popular with German printers. $35-40.

Extremely bright German 4" X 7" pull-downs in popular themes. $20-25 each.

Right: German pull-down, 4" X 7", a very popular 5 cent card of which thousands were produced. $15-20.

Above: German 2" X 3" pull-downs from 1935 collection. $5-7 each.

German 4" X 5" pull-downs marked "2 for 5 cents." $7-10 each.

Right: Medium sized German pull-downs, 5" X 6." $10-15 each.

Left: German 4" X 7" pull-downs printed on unusually thick cardboard stock in garden themes. $20-25 each.

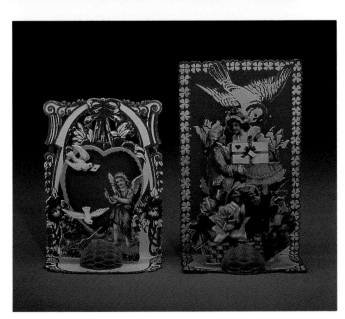

Above: Variety of more expensive German pull-downs, all of which are deeply embossed for this period. $20-25 each.

Left: German 4" X 6" pull-downs marked "1932" on backs. $5-10 each.

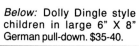

Left: Variety of small German pull-downs sold in sets for school exchange. $3-5 each.

Below: Dolly Dingle style children in large 6" X 8" German pull-down. $35-40.

Above: Medium sized German transportation-themed valentines. $25-30 each.

Right: Popular box style standing valentines used often as place cards at Valentine's Day parties. $10-15 each.

136

Large and small valentines incorporating honeycomb continued to be produced. Red was invariably the only color used for honeycomb. The colors of the valentines also became extremely bright, most likely in an attempt to produce valentines which would attract the customer from a distance when displayed on shelves.

Large 8" X 14" with Grace Drayton type children doing their Valentine laundry. $40-50.

German fold-out, 6" X 11" lighthouse, with small honeycomb decoration behind boat. $15-20.

Large 14" X 8" honeycomb boat with easel back and mechanical boy with oar in hand. $50-60.

Three examples of honeycomb valentines, the rarest to the left with pastel honeycomb not typical of this decade. $20-30 each.

Variety of German cards illustrating creative uses of honeycomb as decorative effect. $10-15 each.

Four styles of American cards with honeycomb attachments. $10-20 each.

Large 8" X 14" in popular circus theme. $40-50.

Two large 6" X 9" American honeycomb cards. $10-12 each.

German-manufactured mechanical valentines continued to be produced in prolific quantities, but the size of them declined in an attempt to sell them by the set to parents of school children who would subsequently exchange them with their entire class. Thus, valentines were downsized in an attempt to compete with American mechanicals which could be sold far more inexpensively. There were some larger style mechanicals still made for those children who could afford more, with most of these primarily marketed on the East Coast.

Small German mechanical valentines sold in sets for school exchange. $2-5 each.

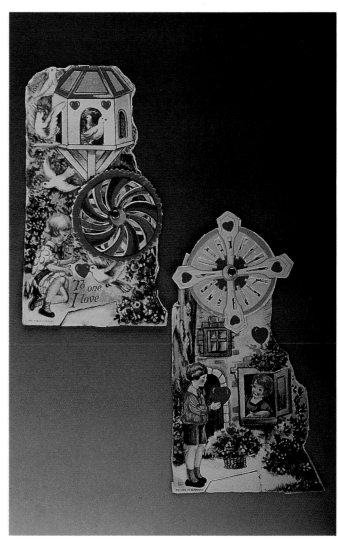

Above: Larger German mechanicals
with revealing wheels, both of which
were given to a teacher. $10-12 each.

Left: Medium sized exchanged
in a rural Kansas school in 1934.
$1-3 each.

Medium sized German mechanicals exchange in 1934 in rural Kansas country school. $1-3 each.

Smaller German mechanicals with very cleverly devised moving parts. $3-5 each.

German mechanicals with moving eyes. $3-4 each.

Above, left: Large 6" X 8" German mechanicals with elaborate moving parts. $5-7 each.

Above, right: Animal themed German mechanicals. $5-7 each.

Left: Large 8" X 10" German mechanicals with moving wheel-turned action. $15-20 each.

Simple little German printed cards continued to be marketed, especially as part of sets. Invariably these cards were retailed as "two for five cents" or even "three for five cents" as Valentine's Day drew near. These cards were the mainstay of many a five and dime or variety store in this decade.

Small 3" German fold-over cards. $1-2 each.

Medium sized 4"X 5" German flats with easels. $1-3 each.

Variety of small German
fold-over cards. $1 each.

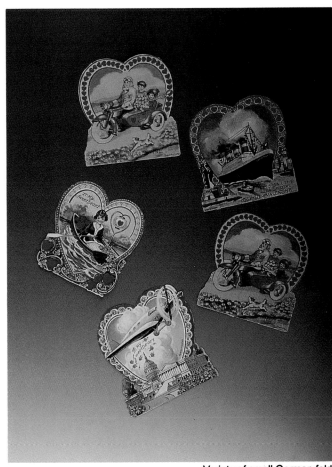

Variety of small German fold-over cards, more rare since transportation themes are used. $1-2 each.

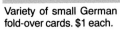

Small 3" simple on outside German fold-over. Inside reveals quite elaborate fold-down scene.$3-5.

Whitney continued to produce some very elegant valentines. During this particular period Whitney downsized many of their cards in a time when more expensive cards were not in vogue. Whitney continued to use lace and chromolithographs, but on smaller cards so they could be sold more inexpensively.

Above: Medium sized 4" square Whitney cards still incorporating lace on outside of card. $1-2 each.

Above: Small Whitney fold-over cards sold in sets for school exchange. $1 each.

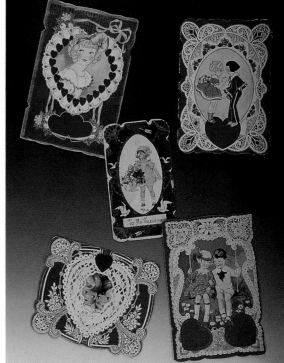

Above: More expensive Whitney cards sold in sets for school exchange. $1-3 each.

Left: Least expensive Whitney cards sold in sets for school exchange. $1 each.

145

Americans Continue to Move into Valentine Card Ventures

American Greetings started manufacturing valentines in this decade. Its history began in 1906, when 22-year-old Jacob Sapirstein, nicknamed "J.S.," began a card wholesaling business in his Cleveland home and sold postcards from a horse-drawn wagon. J.S.'s sons, 9-year-old Irving in 1918 and later, Morris in 1926, joined the business to sell cards for their father. By 1932 J.S. began producing his own cards, and the company hired its first sales person in 1934. A third son joined the family business in 1935, and the company opened a branch in Detroit in 1936. The name American Greetings Publishers was adopted in 1940, the year the company's sales first topped one million dollars. Cards of this period mostly sold for one to five cents, with the most expensive cards going for ten cents.

Hallmark, located in Kansas City, Missouri, moved into a new six-story building in 1936. Several years later, they soon outgrew this facility and an even larger building was acquired. In 1955, a unique seven-story building was built into a hill with the building constructed in such a manner that there are street entrances to each floor and a bridge over one street connecting with the older factory. Even the roof was utilized with parking for over 600 cars. Various American manufacturers produced mechanical and flat valentines, all of which are marked "Made in U.S.A."

American comic with fold over flap changing facial expression. $5-7.

American flats in Art Deco style. $2-3 each.

American winter-theme valentines from 1938. $1-2 each.

American valentines incorporating very inexpensive honeycomb which quickly faded. $2-5 each.

Simple American valentines, with some very creative design and verses. $1-3 each.

American novelties with attached foil mirrors. $3-5 each.

Below: American valentines with honeycomb with more desirable themes and designs. $2-5 each.

Above: American valentines with honeycomb with more creative themes. $2-6 each.

Some of the most desirable valentines for collectors are those which reflect social history, especially those which illustrate comics characters, cartoon personalities, or famous people of American life. Since the moving picture had become ingrained in American life and more leisure time was available, innumerable personalities arose and were subsequently recorded in valentine history. What follows is a brief look at some of the important personalities of this decade.

Disney Valentines

Mickey and Minnie Mouse

Walt Disney started his lucrative business of animating figures on film with a collaborator, Ubbe Iwerks. Like all beginners, Disney needed a special figure and he found Mickey Mouse, who debuted in 1928. Artless and awkward, he squeaked in shrill tones in the early talkies. Shortly after the release of his highly successful film, postcards bearing his image appeared. Mickey has become the most recognized and celebrated cartoon character in history. In 1938, Valentine and Sons, Ltd. printed a series of valentines which were copyrighted. These mechanical cards included themes such as Mickey dancing in a hula skirt and Mickey as a tailor posing with Minnie in medieval costume. Hall Brothers (later known as Hallmark) produced fold-over cards incorporating different themes with Mickey and Minnie as well as stylized cut-out, free-standing characters.

Variety of American valentines incorporating cartoon mice as themes. $5-7 each.

Snow White and the Seven Dwarfs

When this animated classic appeared, valentines were quickly marketed. While many different variations were produced, most were sold in varying sizes of sets. One set of eight cards included the seven dwarfs, each in a classic pose identifying them with either a musical instrument or prop which moved via a rivet, thus creating a mechanical card. Another set of three cards copyrighted in 1938 by Walt Disney Enterprises included two scenes from outside the dwarfs' cottage with the door opening to reveal an interior resulting from a tab which pushed in and locked the valentine into a three-dimensional, free-standing card. A third set of four-heart shaped, mechanical cards is copyrighted 1938 by W. D. Ent. In one card Snow White is awakened by the seven dwarfs who "pop" up and down when a tab is pulled. In another, Dopey mechanically "peeks" in the door. Another has Snow White dancing with Grumpy. One features Snow White baking a pie out of which two birds "rise" with love greetings.

Set of three mechanical free-standing valentines push in tab revealing interiors. $85-95.

Right: Complete set of Snow White and Seven Dwarfs mechanicals from 1938. $75-85 each valentine.

Far right: Set of four mechanical Snow White valentines from 1938. $50-75 each.

Released as a movie in February, 1940, Walt Disney introduced Pinocchio valentines in advance of the movie opening. Therefore, these cards were copyrighted in 1939 by Walt Disney Productions. A variety of different mechanical cards was produced which commemorated this very famous cartoon and movie star character. One illustrates Geppetto (bending up and down) seeking Pinocchio on a home-crafted raft. Still another illustrates Pinocchio at a circus with a donkey (kicking up and down) and a merry-goround. One mechanical features a horse-drawn coach inside of which Jiminy Cricket sits (bouncing up and down with the bumps in the road). Other cards featured the wiley fox, the fairy, Gideon, and other characters contained in the movie.

Pinocchio mechanical from 1939. $55-65.

Two Pinocchio mechanical valentines from 1939. $55-65.

Maggie, of Jigs and Maggie Valentine—popular Sunday comics personalities. $40-50.

Variety of comic cartoon and comic strip characters from 1930s. $20-30 each.

Alice in Wonderland valentine produced in different styles—mechanical, flat, and easel backed. $20-25.

Since many of these valentines were purchased by children and given to their friends, it is important to get a sense of some of the customs of this decade. Some of those customs have been recorded in various journals and magazines. *School Arts*, an educational aids magazine for teachers, often documents valentine customs as celebrated by our youth. In 1935 Edith McCoy, an art teacher from Newark, Ohio, recounted the fact that her students loved St. Valentine's Day the best of all holidays, even over Christmas. "They get a great many thrills when making their love missives; more thrills when their handicraft is sent to little friends, doting grandparents, and other fond relatives, with a grand climax on February fourteenth when the Valentine Box in their schoolroom is opened and little postmen deliver its contents."

McCoy carefully illustrates and explains instructions for creating cut-paper hearts of varying degrees to be created by students in grades two to six. "Art for life's sake is the aim of art in the public schools," according to McCoy who spent weeks preparing valentines with her students. February was the party month and *St. Nicholas* magazine was very willing to describe some party ideas for parents and young readers. A "Cupid's Air-Mail Party." Even the invitation's wording was suggested:

LIKE POPEYE LOVES HIS SPINACH
LIKE MICKEY LOVES HIS MIN,
THAT'S HOW I'D LOVE TO HAVE YOU
ON VALENTINE'S—DO COME IN!

NAME: DATE: HOUR:

The author, H.C.M., went on to suggest, "When the guests arrive, give each one a postman's cap and a mail sack. When all are there, one person plays Cupid and stands in the center of a circle. Cupid gives each person the name of a city. Then he shouts 'Mail from New York to Denver!' or whatever cities he has named. The guests having these names fly with airplane speed to change chairs. While they are changing, Cupid tries to get one of the chairs. The person left without a chair becomes Cupid. Further suggestions included valentine fortune telling, setting the table in pink and white, and a menu including tomato bouillon, creamed chicken in heart-shaped patty shells, pink ice-cream hearts or cupid parfait, and cocoa with marshmallow. Even recipes were included in this February, 1936 article.

In 1938, one popular game played was "The Black Heart." Before school in the morning, the teacher hid hearts cut from construction paper of every conceivable color in the classroom. Each color had a particular significance. Red hearts counted one point, green put the finder in debt by one point, blue gave the finder a prize, and so on. But whoever found the black heart had to pay some terrible forfeit. Usually this student had to clean the blackboard or do some other classroom cleaning. It should be noted that the receiver of the black heart did receive a special gift from the teacher at the end of the day to insure no misgivings on such a wonderful day.

Another popular custom was to give each student the name of a classmate. Then the student was to create a special valentine illustrating this person in one-half hour. For instance, Johnny might be a good egg. Therefore the classmate who drew his name would create a valentine with an egg theme. Then a "Show and Tell" period would follow in which students would explain their artistic renditions and deliver the valentine in front of the class. Refreshments including special cookies, chocolates, and a punch usually followed to close the day.

A glance at some catalog pages from this decade can help to give pricing and availability of various cards and party supplies during this decade. In 1933, David C. Cook's Publishing Company provide such a view.

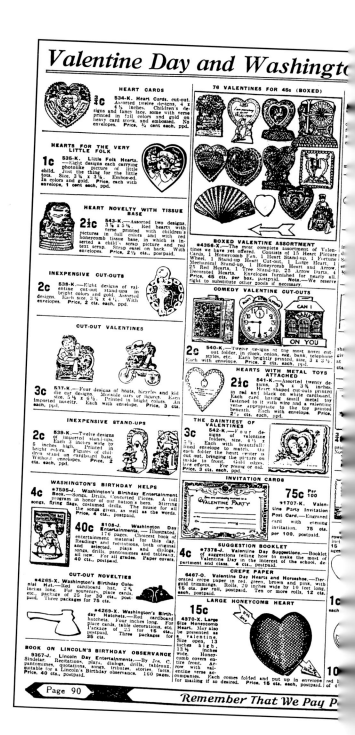

By the end of the decade, cards had changed somewhat and that is reflected from a glimpse of a David C. Cook 1937 catalog.

Many companies were selling more inexpensive American-produced cards in the latter part of this decade for school distribution. Slack Manufacturing Co. of Chicago, Illinois in the 1938 catalog *Favors, Decorations, and Specialties for all Occasions* helps us to see that trend.

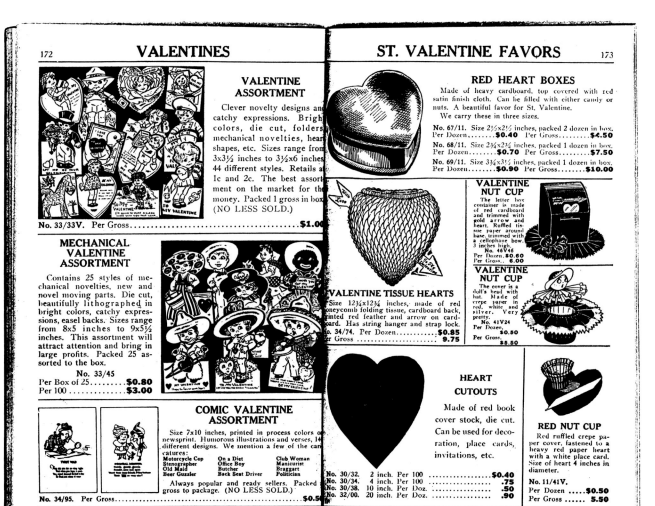

172   **VALENTINES**

VALENTINE ASSORTMENT

Clever novelty designs and catchy expressions. Bright colors, die cut, folders, mechanical novelties, heart shapes, etc. Sizes range from 3x3½ inches to 3½x6 inches. 44 different styles. Retails at 1c and 2c. The best assortment on the market for the money. Packed 1 gross in box. (NO LESS SOLD.)

No. 33/33V. Per Gross..................................$1.00

MECHANICAL VALENTINE ASSORTMENT

Contains 25 styles of mechanical novelties, new and novel moving parts. Die cut, beautifully lithographed in bright colors, catchy expressions, easel backs. Sizes range from 8x5 inches to 9x5½ inches. This assortment will attract attention and bring in large profits. Packed 25 assorted to the box.

No. 33/45
Per Box of 25........$0.80
Per 100 ....$3.00

COMIC VALENTINE ASSORTMENT

Size 7x10 inches, printed in process colors on newsprint. Humorous illustrations and verses, 14 different designs. We mention a few of the card features:

Motorcycle Cop	On a Diet	Club Woman
Stenographer	Office Boy	Manicurist
Old Maid	Butcher	Braggart
Beer Guzzler	Back Seat Driver	Politician

Always popular and ready sellers. Packed gross to package. (NO LESS SOLD.)

No. 34/95. Per Gross...................................$0.50

SLACK MFG. CO.   124-126 W. LAKE STREET CHICAGO, ILL.

ST. VALENTINE FAVORS   173

RED HEART BOXES

Made of heavy cardboard, top covered with red satin finish cloth. Can be filled with either candy or nuts. A beautiful favor for St. Valentine. We carry these in three sizes.

No. 67/11. Size 2½x2½ inches, packed 2 dozen in box. Per Dozen........$0.40   Per Gross.........$4.50
No. 68/11. Size 2¾x2¾ inches, packed 1 dozen in box. Per Dozen........$0.70   Per Gross.........$7.50
No. 69/11. Size 3¾x3½ inches, packed 1 dozen in box. Per Dozen........$0.90   Per Gross.......$10.00

VALENTINE TISSUE HEARTS

Size 12¾x12¾ inches, made of red honeycomb folding tissue, cardboard back, printed red feather and arrow on cardboard. Has string hanger and strap lock.
No. 34/74. Per Dozen...........$0.85
Per Gross 9.75

VALENTINE NUT CUP

The letter box container is made of red cardboard and trimmed with gold arrow and heart. Ruffled tissue paper around base, trimmed with a cellophane bow. 3 inches high.
No. 46V46
Per Dozen, $0.60
Per Gross, 6.00

VALENTINE NUT CUP

The cover is a doll's head with hat. Made of crepe paper in red, white and silver. Very pretty.
No. 41V24
Per Dozen, $0.50
Per Gross, $5.50

HEART CUTOUTS

Made of red book cover stock, die cut. Can be used for decoration, place cards, invitations, etc.

No. 30/32.	2 inch. Per 100	......	$0.40
No. 30/34.	4 inch. Per 100	......	.75
No. 30/38.	10 inch. Per Doz.	......	.50
No. 32/00.	20 inch. Per Doz.	......	.90

RED NUT CUP

Red ruffled crepe paper cover, fastened to a heavy red paper heart with a white place card. Size of heart 4 inches in diameter.
No. 11/41V.
Per Dozen $0.50
Per Gross 5.50

SLACK MFG. CO.   CHICAGO, ILL.

Chapter IX
American Cards Emerge:
1940-1949

These were sad years for many Americans who missed their loved ones fighting in World War II. Although very important for the world, the war still took its toll on the patience and beliefs of individuals and families. Soldiers in a foreign land longed for any word from their families. Card publishers once again went to work as they did during World War I to create classifications of various designs and sentiments suitable to send to those in service. Patriotic designs, obviously, were their first choice. When these did not sell very well, the card manufacturers quickly abandoned patriotic themes but still used red, white, and blue themes. Even these were gradually rejected in favor of old-fashioned designs and themes in the latter part of the war years.

As the war progressed, raw materials became scarce and government restrictions on the use of paper made it imperative to curtail card manufacturing. Citizen committees as well as card manufacturer representatives bombarded Washington to lobby the lessening of the restrictions, claiming that cards were morale builders for our troops overseas. At times, they were successful, but with the increasing demand for cards, the shortages continued. Even more scarce are valentines sent from overseas by our military.

While the war raged, those on the home front continued to commemorate Valentine's Day with new trends and customs to take our minds off the war. A major industry grew out

Comic valentine printed on heavy paper stock, 4" X 5", late 1930s. $5-7 each.

of Valentine's Day in this decade. Millions of greeting cards, the production of thousands of heart-shaped boxes of candy, and the staging of high school dances helped to fuel the economy. Many of the valentines in 1940 with such titles as "To Someone Sweet" and "Because You're You" were extremely popular. Valentines with perfumed flowers, and hearts scented with old lavender were novelties. In fact some six million dollars was spent on scented hearts according to the February 12, 1940, issue of *Newsweek.*

Due to the war *Recreation* in its February, 1941, issue suggests party invitations be simple, perhaps just in the shape of red or white hearts. As a novelty, it was suggested that "tickets of admission" be presented at the door. The ticket could be a valentine which was collected and placed in a mail box or gaily decorated box at the entrance to the party, for later distribution to hospitals. Heart trees made from bare branches decorated with red and white hearts were suggested. These were to be held in place by "planting" them in sand, soil, or coal—covered up, of course. Silhouettes cut from mat stock or heavy wrapping paper were suggested for the walls. Games suggested include guessing the number of candy hearts in a glass jar, "cupid psycho-analyzer" played by placing fortunes in a large container to be drawn out by guests, and "finding the way to your heart" played by blindfolding players and giving them gold paper-covered keys to place on a large red heart in the center of which is a key hole. These were played over and again in elementary school classrooms across the country.

Also suggested were circle games of "Heart Condition," "Matching Hearts," and "Mending Hearts" detailed with relays and pencil games. Refreshments of sandwiches cut in heart shapes and spread with strawberry jam and cream cheese, valentine-shaped cookies decorated with red and white frosting, salads with lots of red cherries, gelatins in heart molds, and red fruit punches were possibilities mentioned.

Comic valentines enjoyed a resurgence during this time period, partly due to a need for a sense of humor in some very bad times and partly due to card manufacturers attempting to produce valentines at a lower cost. These simple sheets were perfect alternatives to fold-over and mechanical cards which were more costly to produce. It should be noted that comic valentines of this type were re-introduced in the mid-1930s and gained new status and popularity during the war years.

Set of comic valentines labeled in red ink "Made in U.S.A." on thin paper, 1940s. $5-7 each.

156

Set of comic valentines labeled in red ink "Made in U.S.A." on thin paper, 1940s. $5-7 each.

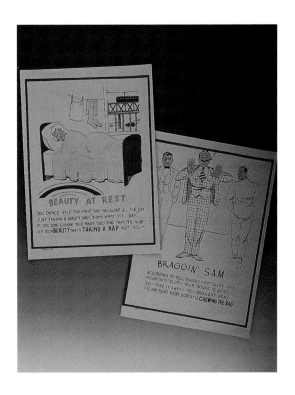

Set of comic valentines labeled in
red ink "Made in U.S.A." on thin
paper, 1940s. $5-7 each.

Set of comic valentines labeled in red ink "Made in U.S.A." on thin paper, 1940s. $5-7 each.

Set of comic valentines labeled in red ink "Made in U.S.A." on thin paper, 1940s. $5-7 each.

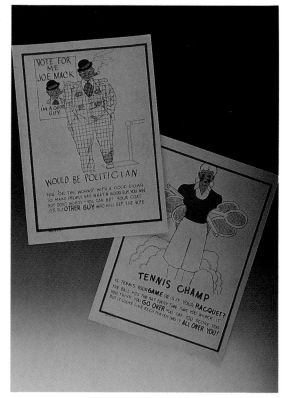

War Boosts Valentine Card Sales

Cecil Inman, of New York, was highlighted in the "Interesting People in the American Scene" feature of *American Magazine* in March 1941, as being the man behind most of the heart throbs and heartaches that Americans have on St. Valentine's Day. He was credited for thinking up over 1,000 ideas a year which went into 75,000,000 valentines each February 14th.

Inman designed his first valentine at the age of five. His next door neighbor, an artist, guided his hand in painting a simple design. It was received so enthusiastically that for years he turned out original valentines for his family and friends. By the 1940s he designed only one personal card a year--a giant valentine, covered with lace, handpainted, and fancy lettering for his wife.

In a personal interview, Inman stated that "Reason is why women buy 90 percent of all valentines sold." Always on the scent for sentiment, he gleaned his ideas from comic strips, animated cartoons, psychology textbooks, tennis matches, and even prize fights. After a fight in 1940, he hurried home and designed a card showing a boxing glove hitting a heart. Under it he wrote, "You simply floor me... You're a knockout."

One development helped the entire industry in some very competitive times. The Greeting Card Association of America was founded in 1941 to help out the industry and companies who produced valentines. Earlier known as "The National Association of Greeting Card Manufacturers," it consisted of almost ninety percent of the firms which produced cards in the United States. When reformed in 1941, it consisted of sixty different firms. The association was composed of three groups: one served the retail stores, one served the wholesalers, and the last one served those whose products were sold to sales representatives selling directly to the consumer.

The 1940s enjoyed the continuation of valentine exchanges in school. As a result, much history was exchanged in a typical classroom of 30 plus students in grades 1-8. Many collections of valentines were saved by teachers who never could throw anything away, especially if it was something given to them by a student. Thus collections owned by a teacher can reveal some interesting trends. One such collection reminds us of the fact that most children's' valentines of this period sold for one to five cents with "Made in U.S.A." the most common marking on the back of the card. Hallmark, Gibson, and American Greeting Co. were manufacturing cards during the 1940s. This more than any other decade contained cards with a true American flavor.

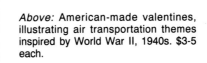

Above: American-made valentines, illustrating air transportation themes inspired by World War II, 1940s. $3-5 each.

Left: American-made valentines, all with war themes, 1940s. $3-6 each.

Right: American-made fold-over cards, all with war themes, 1940s. $3-5 each.

One innovation of this decade was the use of satin puffs, most often appearing as hearts in cards. These pink and red puffs were pioneered by "The Paramount Line," which had its start in 1906. They also sold the first boxed set of valentine cards during World War I. This company was founded by Samuel A. and Charles A. Markoff in Providence, Rhode Island.

American Greeting Co. produced many valentines for the American market during this decade, with their cards being identified with their trademark on the back. At this point in valentine card history, it is virtually impossible to identify every American firm producing valentines in the 1940s. In addition to this, many companies used up to ten different trademarks for their cards, depending upon their final selling destination—be it in a variety store or in a high end department store.

Parchment paper was a favorite in this decade upon which some very art deco-type designs were imprinted. One novelty of this period was to cut out part of the front of the card and place behind it silver or gold foil or upon occasion, thin plastic upon which a lace design was printed, reminiscent of the lacy valentines sent in earlier decades. Stylistic ladies wearing huge hoop skirts and carrying open parasols reflected the women's fashions of the day.

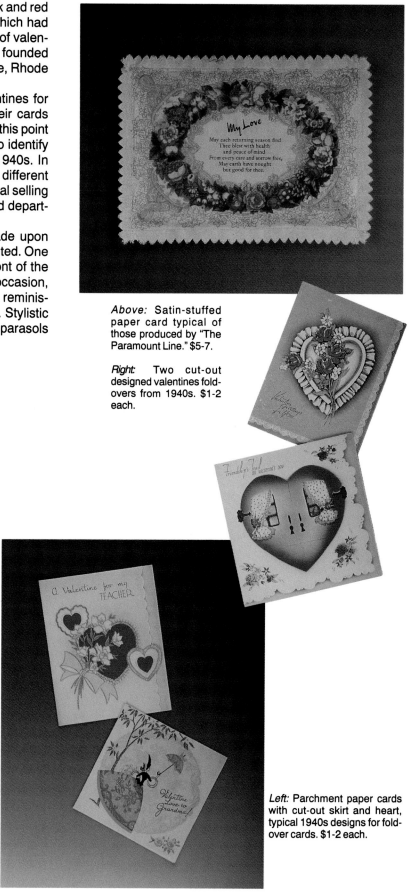

Above: Satin-stuffed paper card typical of those produced by "The Paramount Line." $5-7.

Right: Two cut-out designed valentines fold-overs from 1940s. $1-2 each.

Above: Expensive 5" X 7" boxed musical valentine from 1940s, "Cardoza Buzza." $10-15.

Left: Parchment paper cards with cut-out skirt and heart, typical 1940s designs for fold-over cards. $1-2 each.

Towards the end of the decade cards took on more of a sentimental design, most often incorporating bouquets of roses, daisies, or pansies. Since cards are a reflection of social history, it might be interpreted that Americans coming out of World War II were ready to get back to nature and beauty since flower and garden scenes rather than people were the main designs of most cards manufactured in the late 1940s. A typical verse read,

Just a little word or two,
coming from the
HEART to you
Just to say
I LIKE you—and
In MY opinion
YOU'RE JUST GRAND!

Right: Typical "U.S.A." cards from 1940s. $1-2 each.

Below: Hallmark cards from 1940s decade 1-2 each.

Left: Elaborate 6" square boxed flat valentine with lace. $10-15.

The Fairfield Line appears to begin in the 1940s from the style of the cards found. These often have cut open hearts revealing lined or full foil hearts with printed greetings and the use of ribbons which was revitalized as a part of card designs in the early part of this decade. Ribbons, feathers, and even little sentiments such as plastic wishbones, spoons, and medals were often added to cards in an attempt to produce cards which would attract the attention of people use to lacy and fold-out valentines still popular at the start of World War II. These cards were a further reaction to thousands of simple flat valentines printed by American card companies in the 1930s.

Above: Attached coat hanger typical of Fairfield Line. $5-7.

Left: Applied foil mirror typical of Fairfield Line. $3-5.

Right: Left-over German stock sold at start of World War II in Milwaukee variety store. $1-3 each.

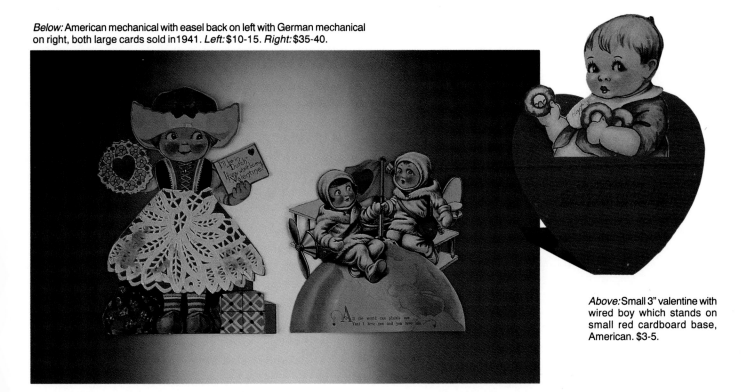

World War II resulted in increased sales of valentines with a record-breaking demand that depleted supplies long before February 14 in 1945. In 1944, the trade grossed over 55 million dollars. St. Valentine's Day cards were now second to Christmas in sales. Retail prices ranged from five cents for the heart-shaped kind exchanged in school to $5 for the elaborate, hand-made creations. Women bought 85 percent of all greeting cards, and a majority of those cards were sent to servicemen abroad.

A variety of war-themed cards appeared including a Wac holding an official card with this verse, "Be my Valentine... It may not be official business, But I hope you know— Next to Uncle Sam, you're my official beau." Sailors on ships, army boys in gunner tanks and standing at attention with a gun--all of these cards reflected a time when much sadness was taking place, but also a time to remember loved ones who just might not be there next Valentine's day. The war caused most verses to be less sentimental and more directed to keeping spirits up in a time when families could not be together.

During World War II, Beistle of Shippensburg, Pennsylvania ceased the manufacturing of honeycomb. Material shortages eliminated their ability to make items, and their inventory was soon depleted.

In 1949 over 300,000,000 cards were sold and sent. With over 175,000,000 sales for American greeting card manufacturers in this year, ten percent of this business was attributed to valentines sales. Jewelers, confectioners, and especially florists also rejoiced as 390,748 roses were sold. Confectioneries reported a ten percent increase in sales over 1948 and jewelers reported over 190,000,000 dollars was spent on jewelry during February. Obviously this was a lucrative time period for all three of these major industries in this country as Americans more and more turned to celebrate Valentine's Day with gusto.

Unfortunately, the war took its toll on American and European valentine manufacturers. The corporations of Raphael Tuck and George C. Whitney were liquidated in 1942 due to war shortages. The critical paper shortage imposed due to the war forced Warren Whitney to close his family business. It was especially difficult for Whitney because this one family business had been operational for 77 continuous years. Their presses, stock on hand, and good will were sold to a Chicago- based business, Carrington, specializing in color printing. Subsequently, this business was liquidated and sold to a Worcester , Massachusetts concern. Unfortunately most of the old plates were lost in the 1910 fire, and this new generation did not save as much as the previous generation. Thus much company history was lost.

Anti-German sentiment forced the Hebrew Publishing Company to sell its Littauer & Boysen inventory. It is recorded that Dennison sold leftover L&B paper dolls and valentines in the basement of its New York store. Much of the stock from the Hebrew Publishing Company found its way into the shop of Arthur Brandon, who opened a store on 64th Street in New York during World War II with a huge consignment of old scrap he had purchased from them for a very small amount of money. No one wanted merchandise with "Made in Germany" imprinted on it. Much artistry and creative design were lost forever, never to be fully recovered in the valentine card industry.

Right: German printed mechanicals sold in early war years in Oshkosh, Wisconsin department store. $1-3 each.

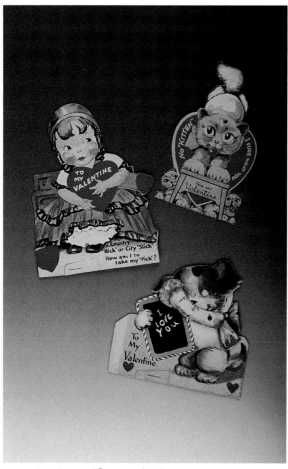

Above: American and German printed mechanicals sold at start of World War II. $1-3 each.

Above: Small 3" valentine with wired goose which stands on small white cardboard base, American. $3-5.

Left: American-made card with heart base and collapsible house attached. $10-15.

Above and right: Closed American comic fold-out valentines in large 12" X 13" sizes. Opened cards reveals comic characters . $7-10 each.

Opened American cards revealing verses and themes.

Closed 12" X 6" American fold-down valentines. $5-7 each.

Left: American card inspired by comic strip popularity of this decade. $7-10.

Right: Comic fold-over card inspired by comic strip and radio popularity of "Terry and the Pirates." $12-15.

Left: Peek-a-boo mechanical cards, American. $3-5 each.

Large 12" American mechanicals which were priced at 5 cents in 1948. $10-12 each.

Large 7" X 9" mechanical cards with tabs. $4-6.

Elegant large 14" X 12" American valentine with foil window and easel back. $5-10.

Large 8" X 13" mechanical with mailbox which opens to reveal inserted miniature greeting card. $15-20.

Right: All larger American mechanicals with easel backs. $3-5 each.

Far right: Variety of small sized mechanicals sold in sets for school exchange parties. $1-3 each.

Far left: Large mechanical valentines produced and sold in 1948. $3-5 each.

Left: Variety of Carrington cards with easel backs. $2-3 each.

171

Left: Variety of small sized Carrington cards sold in sets. $1-3 each.

Left: Easel backed valentines illustrating our new-found fascination with telephone during war years. $3-5 each.

Above: Variety of small flats illustrating musical themes and marked "1944" on backs. $1-2 each.

172

Above: Variety of small flats illustrating musical themes. $1-3 each.

Right: Small inexpensive set of valentines which sold for 19 cents. $1-2 each.

173

Right: Large valentines which sold for 5 cents each in 1948. $3-6 each.

Above: Cowboy themes so popular at end of 1940s. $3-7 each.

Right: American-printed black-themed valentines, the middle one of which is mechanical. $10-15 each.

174

Variety of cards showing various
modes of transportation in 1940s.
$1-3 each.

Fantasy-themed cards illustrating
imaginative methods of delivering
valentine greetings. $1-2 each.

Typical 1940s styles of fold-over cards. $1 each.

American fold-over cards, two bottom of which have easel backs. $1-2 each.

Simple American mechanicals
from late 1940s. $1-2 each.

Larger 1940s styles of fold-over
cards with front part being cut
out. $1-2 each.

Left: Simple 2 cent cards produced by Hallmark. $1-2 each.

Above: Simple flat cards sold in 1949. $1 each.

Left: Typical 1940s cards including war themes from mid part of World War II. $1 each.

178

Chapter X
Children's Cards Proliferate:
1950-1959

The period after World War II saw a new tide of prosperity and national pride sweeping the nation. Americans no longer looked to Europe for valentine cards nor did we care for the sentimental themes of old. As a result, American companies dominated the valentine card market. While children continued to exchange and send cards, adults abandoned this custom somewhat. Part of the reason lies in an attempt to discard tradition and seek new customs. While Valentine's Day continued to be extremely important, the sending of cards dwindled when Americans turned to sending flowers and boxes of candy to their sweethearts. Heart-shaped boxes profusely decorated with satin, ribbon, and flowers dominated the market. In fact, many card manufacturing companies turned to producing these heart-shaped boxes to survive in a period when this was the rage.

Some traditionalists, however, still clung to card sending. Therefore, American printers needed to supply cards which reflected new social customs and decorating styles. Whitman Publishing Company of Racine, Wisconsin, is a recognized name in children's books. Many collectors came to recognize Whitman also as a large manufacturer of valentines, especially the inexpensive ones often exchanged by school children. In 1929 Western Publishing Company purchased the Stationer's Engraving Company, which produced engraved stationery and greeting cards. For two years the company remained headquartered in Chicago, but it was moved to Racine and consolidated with the Whitman Publishing Company, a wholly owned subsidiary of Western. In 1931 their Greetings Card Division was started and was headed by Myron O. Lawson, who brought to this position over twenty years of experience.

Lawson's experience in design, color, and plate making in Western's Photo Engraving Department helped to put Whitman in one of the top positions as a greeting card manufacturer. By 1956, Lawson had become one of the top greeting card executives in the country, and he had built the Whitman line to a volume of over 120 million cards a year.

Whitman started producing valentines in the early 1950s. All of their cards were designed by freelance artists who submitted sketches to the Greeting Card Division for approval. Verses for the valentines were selected in the same manner. Once designed, cards were printed by the offset lithographic process on huge printing presses which reproduced full-color illustrations in one step while moving through the presses.

Whitman's line was specifically intended for the low-end market. Most of the cards were sold by the box in "Five and Dime" stores such as Kresge's and Woolworth's. Kits were also produced which allowed children (and adults as well) to make their own cards by cutting out the designs and gluing the individual pieces together. When cards were sold individually, they retailed at four for five cents or two for five cents, depending upon the size of the card.

Typical sentimental themed fold-over cards from this decade. $1-2 each.

Fold-over cards saved from 1956 by teacher in rural Wisconsin school. $1-2 each.

Left: Coloring book valentine card made by Carrington. $10-15.

As the proofer received these sheets of metal, he proofed the yellow first, following with each subsequent color used. The designs selected for the form, together with verses and titles, were photo-composed on a sheet of glass as large as the sheet of paper to be used. When every detail was lined up, the sheets of glass, one of each color, were placed in vacuum frames and everything was transferred to zinc or aluminum by a photographic process. Once the sheets were deep etched, the plates were ready for the printing process.

After the yellow "plate" was transferred and prepared, it was clamped around a cylinder on a large fast-running press. These offset presses consisted of three cylinder rollers. One contained the "plate," the second contained the rubber blanket, and the third contained the impression cylinder, which contained the grippers for carrying the sheets of paper. When form rollers charged with ink rolled over the plate, the printing process commenced.

Eventually inflation brought an end to the Whitman Publishing Company. Cards such as those sold by Hallmark could be sold for a quarter in gift shops while Whitman cards of the same quality had to be priced for a nickel or a dime at variety stores where they were mostly marketed. As a result, the profit margin quickly dwindled and greeting card production was discontinued in the early 1960s.

Now that the four-color plate process was in full use in the printing industry, it is interesting to note how valentines were produced in the 1950s. This is an era when printing expanded and mechanized in so many ways.

One popular, but expensive card was the card with a real etching reproduced on it. Such cards were stamped from copper plates on which the artist had spread a coating of "etching ground." On this surface, he scratched his drawing. Following that, the plate was immersed in an acid which ate into the copper only where the lines of the drawing were. The sketched plate was then steel faced to stand up under continuous printing. If color was applied, it was done by hand. Thus these cards were quite expensive.

But the most common method used was offset printing in four colors: black, yellow, blue, and red. Frequently, other colors were added to produce special effects. First, the original sketch by the artist was photographed "down" to the proper size required for the card through a fine screen, and filters were used to separate the different colors. The subsequent negatives were retouched by a lithographic artist and then printed on a thin sheet of aluminum or zinc, which was then treated with chemicals. Once inked up, it was ready for the proofer. Each separate color had to go through the process.

Two simple valentines exchanged by teacher and pupil, and who were mother and daughter. $1-2 each.

180

Once passed through the press, these sheets were deposited in large piles on trucks so they could easily be rolled from one end of the press to the other for each color. After all the colors were completed and perfectly dry, the sheets were sent to the cutting department. Large cutters then cut them into single cards, ready for the finishers. Once separated, the cards were stacked for inspection. Next, came the folding, for which complicated folding machines were created. If there were any attachments such as ribbon, sachets, satin, or other additions, the cards went to a separate processing department. After passing inspection for the last time, the cards were ready to be boxed and sent to wholesalers.

Since the majority of valentines produced in the 1950s were specifically meant for children, designs and themes reflect this fact. Cut animals in bright and gay colors and brightly dressed children abound with short, to the point, and easy to read verses. Most of these verses were humorous. The better publishers set and maintained high, good-taste standards with their lines.

Assortment of valentines from every major American company producing valentines. $1-2 each.

Very creative verses on larger style cards. $1-2 each.

One popular way to exchange valentines was recorded in *Recreation* in 1953. The teenage club of Parkland Recreation Center in Louisville, Kentucky hit upon the idea of a special delivery valentine mail service, complete with postmaster, clerks, and delivery men. The teens constructed a counter complete with window and slit for inserting valentines. Outgoing and incoming stations were set up at either end. Silver paper with gold-glittered cupids, twisted swirls of red and white crepe paper, and a midnight blue background ablaze with twinkling red hearts were the decorative effects chosen for the post office.

Once the office was ready, the work force went about their duties. The postmaster "barked" instructions, three female clerks sorted by name nearly four hundred valentines, and three other clerks personally delivered the cards through the window to two mailmen who delivered the mail throughout the center. During this time, the eagerly awaiting recipients played festive games and indulged in refreshments. The postal service was such a success that it was continued in succeeding years and expanded even to other holidays such as Easter, Christmas, 4th of July, and even Halloween.

In the February, 1959, issue of *Recreation,* some very intriguing ideas for Valentine's Day parties were promoted. One party idea included hiding short lengths of strings throughout the party hall and then choosing partners with whom to go "hunting." Couples tied strings together as they found them. Couples having the longest string at the end of a given period would then have the longest life of happiness—together.

A relay game with girls lining up in two or more teams at one end of the room, and the boys in the same way at the other end was a second suggestion. Each girl was given a red cloth heart and three pins. At the signal the first girl in each team ran to the first boy in the team opposite and pinned the heart patch on his sleeve. As soon as it was on, she ran back and touched the next in line who ran over and pinned her patch on the next boy in line. As each constantly either pinned the patch on or had it pinned on, they went to the foot of the line.

Animal themed cards from late 1950s. $1-2 each.

Mechanical cards, the tabs of which push up an attachment which reveals hidden messages. $1-2 each.

A third idea was to play "Lover's Fun" in which a string was strung across the room about six feet from the floor. Paper hearts were suspended from the wire at different heights. The guests paired up for the game, and the object was to have the girls "snip hearts from the sky." A girl was blindfolded and turned around three times. In one hand she held a pair of scissors, in the other the end of a piece of string about two feet in length. Her partner held the other end of the string and tried to guide her to a heart by the movement of the string.

The end of the party was devoted to refreshments and the exchanging of valentines, many of which were honeycomb decorated according to the various articles devoted to card exchanges of this decade. These honeycomb-decorated cards continued to be popular as many American companies incorporated honeycomb into their various designs.

Immediately after the War, Beistle of Shippensburg, Pennsylvania expanded its production of honeycomb. Soon other firms began making such honeycomb tissue and incorporated it into their valentines, including Hallmark. Hallmark started producing honeycomb in 1959 and continues to do so today. In addition, Metex of Canoga Park, California started producing honeycomb in 1951 and continues to do so today as well.

182

Large free-standing card exchanged in 1951 in a rural Princeton, Wisconsin school. $5-7.

Above: Large 5" X 8" with girl who stands on circular base when bottom green flaps are fold back. $2-3.

Right: Large 6" X 9" mechanical with easel back. $2-3.

Large valentines with felt attachments and easel backs. $1-3 each.

Large free-standing valentines sold in 1950. $2-3 each.

Large 6" X 9" mechanical trunk which reveals treasure chest of jewels and valentine verse. $3-5.

Cinderella valentine booklet with four pages of verses inside. $5-7.

Mechanical on which the daisy petals reveal hidden verse when moved, 5" X 6". $3-5.

Variety of small valentines
exchanged in 1953. $1 each.

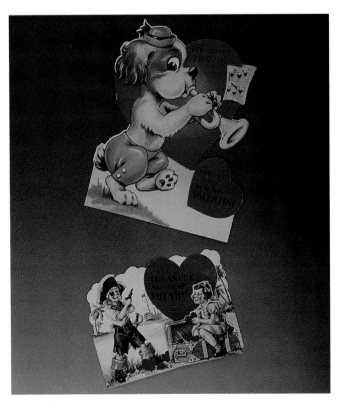

Carrington produced free-
standing cards. $1 each.

Transportation themed cards
from 1950s. $1 each.

186

Assortment of Carrington cards sold in sets for school exchanging. $1 each.

Marked "U.S.A." on backs of these free-standing easel backed cards. $1 each.

187

Simple fold-over heart themed valentines. $1-2 each.

One teacher's assortment saved from her classroom in Green Lake, Wisconsin in 1955. $1 each.

Children's valentines sent in 1958 to a young pre-school boy by his godfather and grandmother. $2-3 each.

Assortment of very inexpensive valentines for school. $1 each.

Cards illustrating food and baking themes. $1 each.

Simple fold-over cards made in United States. $1 each.

Inexpensive fold-over cards from Whitman. $1 each.

"U.S.A." valentines combining photography with printed valentines. $1-3 each.

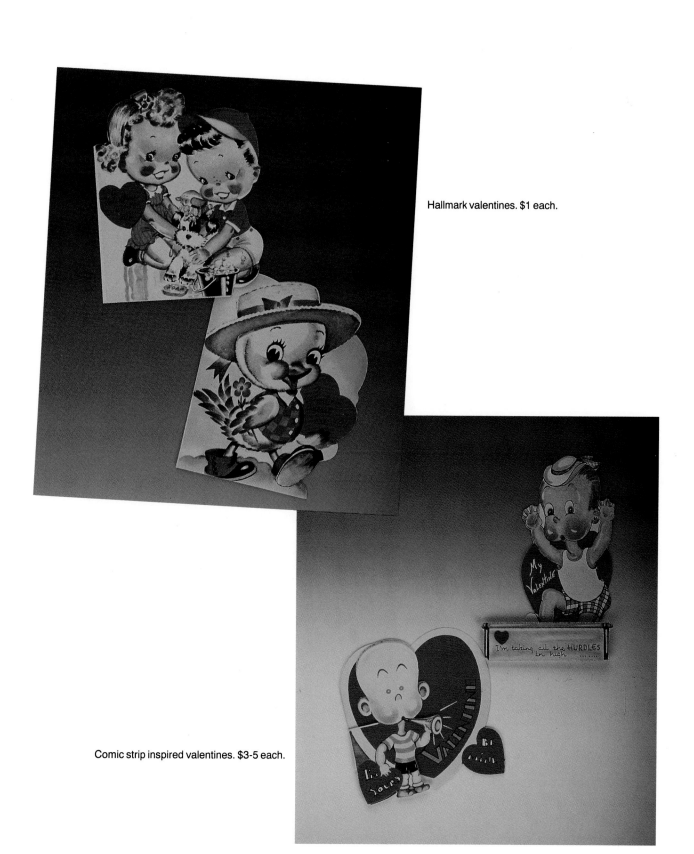

Hallmark valentines. $1 each.

Comic strip inspired valentines. $3-5 each.

Fold-back free-standing cards
exchanged in school. $1 each.

Cards which held sucker, combining
present along with card for school
classmates. $ -2 each.

Chapter XI
Those Simple Years:
1960-1969

This decade was not very significant in that while students continued the tradition of exchanging cards in school, the cards themselves became very simple and inexpensive. Due to fierce competition and the throw-away mentality of our populace, cards were printed on very thin cardboard stock. Today's families were on the move more than ever and found it unnecessary to save anything from the past. Therefore, valentines were almost immediately discarded after they were received. Since so little was saved, card manufacturers quickly picked up on this trend and produced cards in smaller sizes as well as cards with simplistic designs.

Sending heart-shaped boxes decorated with satin ribbons continued to be a popular alternative to sending valentines in the 1960s. The boxes continued to be quite elaborate, and plastic flowers often were incorporated onto the top of the box.

Many sweethearts and married people exchanged gifts. A woman might give a man a book or even socks with hearts printed on them. Red roses were the favorite gift for a man to give a woman.

Some traditions and designs for cards grew out of American comic strips and their artists. Bill Adler in *Good Housekeeping*, February 1967, presented some loving quips and verses in an article entitled "Young Hearts and Valentines." Some favorites included the following:

Dear Eugene,
Will you be my valentine?
Put an X on the blackboard
during recess if the answer is
yes.
Laura

To Ralph:
Your face is funny
Your legs are skinny
You're really not much
But what you got is
okay for Ginny.
Happy Valentine,
Ginny

Dear Richard,
 I am sorry. This is the last
valentine I will send you.
I can't love you any more.
I have a dog now.
Your ex-girl friend,
Marsha

Some of the giants in the card industry continued to produce sets of valentines as well as individual cards most often sold in card and other specialty shops. Cleveland-based American Greetings continued to prosper and grow. In 1960 Irving Stone (all three sons of the Sapirstein family had changed their last names to Stone) was named president and J.S. became chairman. The next year the company opened a plant in Arkansas. Employment grew to over 6,000 in 1966, and plants were opened in Kentucky in 1967 and 1969. In 1967 Holly Hobbie made her first appearance on valentines. In 1968, their sales exceeded $100 million, and the next year the company opened a manufacturing subsidiary in Mexico City.

In 1960, Gibson's company name was changed to Gibson Greeting Cards, Inc., and by 1963, Gibson was reporting sales of more than $26 million dollars. Gibson was involved in foreign language valentines, special designs for supermarkets and discount stores, and a full line of gift wrappings in addition to cards. Gibson common stock was listed on the

New York Exchange in 1963. Two years later, however, Gibson's private ownership ended when the company's assets were purchased by CIT Financial Corporation, as part of that company's plans to expand the scope of its operations. Gibson's product lines continued to expand and facilities were enhanced as plant expansions were carried out along with improvement of the company's production equipmen

Hallmark cards also continued its tradition of providing many artistic and creative cards in this decade. In 1967, Hallmark bought Springbok Editions, a company that manufactured quality jigsaw puzzles, mainly reproductions of fine paintings by such artists as Jackson Pollack, Miro, and Picasso. Therefore, their artistic line greatly expanded with this addition. Joyce C. Hall relinquished his chief executive responsibilities to his son, Donald J. Hall, in 1966. Donald J. Hall is currently chairman of the board.

Other companies continued to produce valentines in a market which became more competitive with each passing year. It should also be noted that the tradition of exchanging valentines also declined towards the end of the 1960s in an era which was marred by the Vietnam Conflict and a youth population that shunned past traditions. Thus many schools abandoned this custom. Only schools in rural areas clung tenaciously to Valentine's Day traditions and card exchanging. Improved communications including the telephone also took its toll on card sending. It was much easier to call someone on Valentine's Day than take the time to choose, address, and send a card.

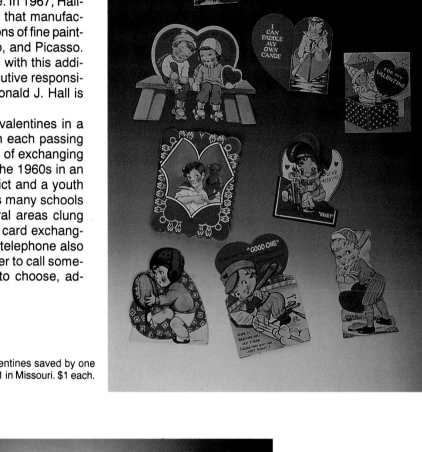

Collection of valentines saved by one little girl from 1961 in Missouri. $1 each.

Stylish dog and cat themed cards typical of 1960s. $1 each.

194

Hallmark card given to teacher in 1964. $1.00

Early 1960s card which contained sucker. $1-2 each.

1965 collection of cards created by
poor school child from his mother's
school day cards. $1.00 each.

Little LuLu card from 1963. $2-3 each.

195

Norcross card given to teacher in 1964. $1.00.

Chapter XII
New Commercial Ventures:
1970-1979

An interesting method of sending valentine greetings started in the early 1970s when newspapers began soliciting their readers to send greetings via the classified ads. *The Cleveland Press CAM*, with Norbert Simpson as their classified ad manager was extremely successful in 1972 in selling such greetings at the rate of one dollar a line. According to Simpson, "An important part of our promotion is a sample selection of various types of messages including sentimental, romantic, serious, and humorous." Appealing to the empathy of their readers, they garnered over three pages of such greetings. His promotion of "Love Notices" not only at Valentine's Day, but at other holidays as well resulted in increased revenues for his newspaper.

The New Britain Herald of Conneticut recorded some very interesting messages sent for Valentine's Day of 1972. There were some tender messages, some beautifully simple, some that brought smiles, and some that evoked mental images of passion.

Among the tender messages:

"RAY, If ever two were one, then surely we. If ever man were loved by wife, then thee. PAT."

"PATRICIA, It's that time of year when I try to compose a special poem, or a gift or some prose, to tell you what you already know. Your valentine's a guy named JOE."

Among the simple messages:

"JOHN, I love you. DIANE"

"DON, I love you now and forever. YOUR VALENTINE."

Among those that piqued interest:

TOMMY, I've been looking around for a while. You've got something for me? A Key? CAROL

MELISSA: Bet you thought I wouldn't do it. Find any more checks? Stay out of trouble and watch the booze. Happy Valentine's Day. CUDDLES

Going public with valentine's greetings continued as a phenomena during the 1970s and gained momentum every year as Americans sought to vent publicly their love for each other. Of course, newspapers continued to promote this fad as it did much for advertising revenues as well as for increased readership of their papers.

GIANTPIE—You're the best Valentine in the whole world. Thanks for being mine. I love you YOUR SHORTCAKE

"Your Shortcake" was one of the over 3000 *New York Post* readers who poured forth their sentiments for Valentine's Day in 1978. Their sugar-coated wishes filled over nine complete pages. Couponed R.O.P. ads ranging from a full page down to 600 lines were the only device used in developing the section. Once again it was indication of the power of display ads put in the newspapers weeks before the day. Probably the most creative was that of a woman who had love in her heart for dozens of "Good Buddies" she talked to on a daily basis over her CB radio on her daily commute on the Long Island Expressway. Her ad took the form of a huge heart filled with such sobriquets as "Sun Bum," "Rust Nail," and "Man from Mars." In the center of the heart was a drawing of the radiator of her car with a license plate that bore her CB identity "SHY 1." At a cost of $300 this Valentine most certainly was on the expensive side.

Other newspapers including the *Chicago Sun-Times* with Don Chalet as advertising manager made "Love" a virtual classified industry in 1978 with 60 solid 8 column tab pages of Valentine's greetings. With over ten thousand ads averaging more than seven lines despite a three line minimum, the *Chicago Sun-Times* more than doubled their 1977 showing of forty pages.

Valentines of this period were much more inexpensive and simple than in previous decades in an attempt to cater to the young who continued to purchase a good portion of cards every season for their classmates. The familiar names continued in this decade. It should be noted that honeycomb was still a popular addition for cards. Devra of Brooklyn, New York, started to produce honeycomb in 1974 and Eureka of Paper Magic in Troy, Pennsylvania, started in 1979. Both companies continue to produce it today. Card companies who incorporated honeycomb onto their cards included American Greetings, C.A. Reed, Gibson, and Hallmark.

The 1970s also went back to the tradition of making your own cards. In a February, 1970, issue of *Harvest Years*, an article entitled "Pretty Personal Valentines" suggested going back to creating a crepe-paper wrapped valentine box. Suggestions were to make personal cards from straw or artificial flowers, or bits of lace—to create the beauty and sentiment of original valentines from years past.

Assortment of cards all marked "1972" on backs. $1.00 each.

Hallmark fold-over card. $1.00.

In the February, 1976, issue of *Seventeen*, it was suggested that paper doilies, plus cutouts, streamers, or bits of ribbon could create a Victorian valentine. To age the card, it was suggested that the paper doilies be dipped in coffee. Other ideas included cutting hearts from red paper, gluing them onto cardboard, and penning an original verse on the card.

There was an attempt to get back to sentiment, especially towards the end of the 1970s. A return to "good old days" with simpler memories soon became a part of card designs. It once again became quite fashionable to send valentines in an era which quickly realized that telephone conversations were temporary whereas cards could be saved and savored time and time again. A renewed interest in greeting cards resulted in the late 1970s when valentines returned to imitate many of the designs used in the early 1900s.

Two 1970s cards. $.50 each.

Sentimental flowers themes revived in mid-1970s. $.50.

199

Hallmark cards from late 1970s. $.50.

Chapter XIII
Into Modern Days:
1980-Present

Valentine history continues to be made. From cards to telegraph to phones to computers, all take their recorded spots as our lives evolve. One new novelty implemented is the computer which many card manufacturers including Hallmark utilized to allow customers to obtain a truly personal card for someone they love. The plunge into Internet communications in the mid-1990s allows Americans to E-mail greetings as well as to electronically choose and send them instantaneously.

For many, the choice still remains to send a valentine greeting through the mail. While most individuals recognize the mainstays of the greeting card industry, many small companies and individuals have begun to provide some individual, creative cards for those who seek the unusual.

Gibson continues to be a familiar giant in the Valentine card business. In 1980, when the RCA Corporation acquired CIT, Gibson became a subsidiary of RCA. Two years later, however, a group of Gibson executives and the Wesray Corporation purchased Gibson from RCA. and in 1983 the name was changed to Gibson Greetings, Inc. when it once again became a publicly owned company. Since then, Gibson has begun to market products including valentines in the United Kingdom and other European countries. Even a Mexican subsidiary was begun to market their line. They further expanded their licenses to include such well-known entertainment industry images such as Sesame Street characters, Disney's Mickey Mouse, and *MAD* magazine characters.

As Gibson moved into the mid-1990s, it experienced several financial challenges. Gibson's Cleo division operated at a loss in 1993. Also during this time, Phar-Mor, Inc., a major retailer of Gibson products, filed for Chapter 11 bankruptcy. In an effort to move into new markets, Gibson acquired The Paper Factory of Wisconsin, Inc. which allowed it to strengthen its position in the booming party products segment of the industry, especially including valentine products. In response to its financial problems, Gibson stepped up efforts to reduce costs. Armed with some hot licensed properties, Gibson plunges ahead in the card market.

A second well-recognized name in the valentine's card market, American Greetings Corporation became one of the world's largest publicly owned manufacturer and distributor in this decade. This company had licenses for Holly Hobbie, Strawberry Shortcake, the Care Bears, Bloomer Bunny, Peppermint Rose, and the Birthday Bear. In 1995, American Greetings had achieved its 89th consecutive year of sales growth and record key measures. Their valentines continue to share a major share of the market place.

A third major player in the valentines market continued to be Hallmark Cards, Inc. In the mid-1990s, a staff of over 700 individuals turned out more than 25,000 greeting cards and other product designs each year. This creative staff is composed of painters, poets, writers, editors, photographers, calligraphers, sculptors, designers, cartoonists, needlework artists and specialists in various graphics techniques. Shoebox Greetings, a division of Hallmark, continued to provide some very witty valentines, reminiscent of those comic valentines of years past.

In 1990, Hallmark introduced "Personalize It!", a line of more than 200 greeting cards enabling customers to incorporate personal information—a nickname, shared joke, or special memory—into pre-written verses via an in-store computer. Consumers also can write their own messages in their valentines. In 1994, Hallmark through its newly established subsidiary, Hallmark Connections ™, began selling personalized greeting cards through on-line and interactive television shopping programs.

The National Stationery Show held in the Jacob Javits Center, New York, from May 15-18, 1993, in its show catalog, listed nearly 160 companies involved in the manufacturing, distribution, and selling of valentines. Hundreds of styles are currently available but many new cards depict designs and replicate artistic cards from the past. Among current popular items are 20 century designs by artists Ellen Clapsaddle, John Winsch, and Ernest Nister, priced from 50 cents to a dollar. More elaborate die-cut cards reproduced from 19th century cards range in price from $1.50 to $5.00. The custom of sending valentines is still firmly established in this country.

Chapter XIV
Tips on Dating Valentines and Making those Minor Repairs

Some Dating Hints

Valentines cover a large span of history. If one wishes to more accurately date items found for sale, there are several factors of which a collector should be aware.

First, examine the valentines. Check the chromolithograph for deep embossing, a sign of an early card. The Germans felt that this deep embossing gave the scraps added beauty and dimension. Also, the earliest of these cards frequently had a gelatin gloss applied over the picture. This gelatin has a tendency to darken over the years, most times giving a slight yellowish cast to the paper. However, it must be noted that valentines were often preserved by gluing them into albums. Therefore, this gelatin coating dissolved and the finish became much more dull in appearance.

As a general rule, highly glossed cards were manufactured before 1900 whereas the full, flat-finished diecuts were manufactured about 1905 to the start of World War I and then after that as well. New scraps also tend to be glossy on both sides. Always carefully examine your card to check for this as well. Newer cards are only lightly embossed.

The weight of the card is important. Old cards tend to employ heavier paper than newer cards. Old scrap tends to be heavier than new, which is printed on very thin paper. In addition, the paper used for the ladders and tabs employed to fold-out the card is much thinner, generally white in color. The older cards will be made of a grayish-yellow paper.

Dark gray or a medium brown indicates the oldest of cards. Deep embossing was generally not employed after Word War I so this would be another indication of age. The colors employed in cards are another key factor when determining the age of a card. When new, many of the old scraps were just as bright as those being printed today. Age has mellowed these colors quite a bit. If the card was kept in an album and protected from the air, the colors might still be quite vibrant. Furthermore, in card manufacturing, each batch may vary in color. So two almost identical cards, made from the same plates but from different runs, may be differently colored. Since prints were pirated, poor printing quality was often a result. Often times, the plates were not accurately placed one on top of each other, and the colors blurred and don't quite match.

This is especially prevalent after World War I. The 20 to 26 color plate process used in the early years added many subtle shades and hues. An absence of this color variation could also indicate a reproduced card since the majority of new chromolithographs being manufactured today use many of the same stamps used years ago. One of the greatest helps in determining the age of a chromolithograph is to examine it with a magnifying glass. New scraps are a screened print which under a magnifying glass will look like newsprint, with only a few tiny, uniformly colored dots. The lithographed paper of long ago under a magnifying glass will display many recognizable dots of different colors.

Subject material is the last consideration when determining the age of a card. Clothing fashions, transportation items, and other such subject material can help to pin down a time frame for valentines. The manufacturer's trademark or other identifying marks can also help. The earliest of cards were unmarked. It seems to be a general rule that those printed before World War I are marked "Germany" whereas those manufactured after World War I are marked "Made in Germany." But that is not a hard and fast rule as stock from before the war was sold in profusion in the United States in the early 1920s after World War I.

Finding an artist's signature is also a help. Then it is possible to date the card, realizing the dates of the artist's life as well as the time the artist was employed by the card manufacturer. Another interesting method is just by determining where the cards were from. How long were they in the family? Some of the greatest finds are often located in the estates of teachers who kept valentines from the beginning of their teaching career right into retirement.

Some Collecting Suggestions

If a valentine has been altered from its original state, that does not necessarily mean that it should be lower in cost. Many valentines have been "doctored" and "repaired" over the years by the recipients or by those who inherited the particular cards. If you wish all original, then obviously some pricing variations might follow. If the valentine is extremely rare or large in size, the pricing will not be affected in any large manner. A 14-inch steam locomotive fold-down with seven layers repaired by gluing the tabs back in place with some minor backing repairs to fragile chromolithographed flowers should not adversely affect price. As long as its integrity as a period piece is kept, it is a valuable treasure.

A badly damaged valentine (unless it is an early Howland or a valentine produced in the industry's infancy stages) with holes, tears, and large stains will not be worth as much as an example in good to pristine condition. However, if it is an extremely rare valentine, it may still be worth it to acquire the valentine rather than not have an example from that time period in your collection. Be wary of purchasing badly damaged valentines from World War I to present times since most of them are quite plentiful.

Invariably an embossed valentine envelope should approximately match in size and design the valentine contained within it. If the envelope being sold with the valentine is much larger or smaller, or has entirely different embossing than the valentine; it may be a replacement, not the original.

Beware of valentines that have a "repackaged" look to them. Be wary of valentines sealed in pictures as they may have been damaged. There is nothing wrong in framing valentines, providing that the purpose of the frame is not to disguise damaged borders or missing backs to valentines.

Keep your valentines in a cool, dry place away from direct sunlight. Acid-free materials would be the best for storing the very expensive, early examples. According to John Schwietzer who gave collecting hints in a newsletter, a Yale University museum curator stated "for every ten degrees that you lower the temperature of your storage area, you potentially double the life of the paper materials stored therein." An old surveyors chest or an old map storage cabinet would be excellent possibilities. Any storage facility with shallow drawers is a good choice since it is dangerous to pile too many valentines upon each other. As the paper ages, it does become brittle at times. In addition, many of the fine, delicate lithographed flowers so fragile at the tips of valentines tend to easily bend. Therefore, it is somewhat dangerous to place to many valentines in one spot. Be careful to arrange them to avoid bending and tearing.

There is nothing wrong with framing valentines in order that they might be enjoyed all year long. However, be careful about placement. Direct sunlight will fade the colors in time. Another tip is to double mat flat pieces to give them a little air which can help prevent the card from getting too brittle over the years and keep the piece from touching the glass. Some individuals use glare-proof glass, but regular glass will do as long as acid free mat board is used for any matting that actually touches the valentine. When double matting, the second one does not touch the valentine so regular mat board may be employed. Be sure to use tiny paper hinges like those used by stamp collectors to attach the valentine to the mat board or fabric backing used.

Repairing Your Valentines

Repairing valentines is a must if they are to be enjoyed by collectors, but extreme caution should be taken to not destroy the integrity and value of the card by following some very basic rules.

Make repairs only with a water soluble glue like Elmer's and be extremely careful to use as little as possible--only enough to make the repair. When scraps have separated or parts broken off, there are two approaches. If the part to be attached is extremely minute and light, cut some tan tissue paper of a size to bridge the two together. Using a toothpick, place a very small amount of glue on the back of both pieces near the tear mark. Join them using the tissue paper. Lightly press the tissue paper to the back of the scrap and let dry. Subsequent layers of tan tissue paper can be used to add strength to the piece.

If the pieces to be combined are large and heavy, it would be best to cut a piece of cardboard to bridge the two together. The best to use would be cardboard or heavy paper somewhat equal to the two pieces being reattached or at the least, a manila file folder-type paper can be used if no old cardboard is available. Carefully put some tiny dots of glue on the piece of cut cardboard. Attach one half to the back of one of the pieces to be combined and press lightly. Wait about one minute and then carefully place the other piece of scrap in place. If tiny bits of cardboard show at the seam, carefully dab them with a bit of glue to seal and bring the colors together. Let dry for several hours and the valentine should be fine.

Since paper honeycomb was originally manufactured as an inexpensive item, it quickly was damaged through the careless opening and closing of cards. Damaged or collapsed cells can be straightened out by carefully reopening the body with a pencil or even a hickory nut pick (the thinner the stylist the better). Open each cell very carefully and then reclose the card and put under a heavy weight or use a large paper clip for smaller pieces.

Allow the card to rest as such for at least a week. If cells need to be re-glued, use the smallest amount of Elmer's glue and use the tip of a large stick pin to apply the glue in tiny dots along the lines to be rejoined. Use extreme caution to use tiny "flecks" of glue or the glue will saturate the layers of tissue, creating a solid mass rather than the original cellular form. Reclose the card and **do not** weight the valentine. This will also help to insure a proper joining.

If scraps are missing, be careful to replace a pre-1900 scrap with one of similar age. This is important historically so that the integrity of the original card is maintained while you as the present owner continue to enjoy the card's beauty. Collectors have a responsibility to maintain the historicity of their cards as new owners will come along as we pass into those times where our collections stay behind. We must be responsible owners so that continuing generations will enjoy the artistry of the past.

Collector's Group for Valentines

Since 1977, a collector's group has existed for those interested in valentines and their collecting. Founded by Evalene Pulati, this group currently includes a very informative quarterly newsletter, a directory which lists members, and a national gathering each year for those interested in this collecting field. In addition, a members' auction is part of the quarterly newsletter. Information and membership can be gained by writing:

National Valentine Collector's Association
Evalene Pulati, newsletter editor
P. O. Box 1404
Santa Ana, California 92702

In an attempt to continue the research of valentines and their manufacturing, the author is interested in hearing from anyone who can help with corrections regarding material contained in this book as well as information for future historical works on this subject. There is much American company history from World War I to present times that remains unrecorded due to various reasons. Of particular interest is the manufacturing of cards in this country. Therefore, any information would be greatly appreciated. The author may be reached at:

Robert Brenner
316 West Main Street
Princeton, Wisconsin 54968
Phone: 414-295-3009
Fax: 414-295-0269
E-mail: rbrenner@mailwiscnet.net

Bibliography

Allen Alister and Joan Hoverstadt. *The History of Printed Scraps*. London:New Cavindish Books, 1983.

Brenner, Robert. *Christmas through the Decades*. Atglen, PA: Schiffer Publishing, 1993.

Buday, George. *The History of the Christmas Card*. London: Spring Books, 1954.

Chase, Ernest Dudley. *The Romance of Greeting Cards*. Cambridge, Mass: Rust Craft,1956.

Fendelman, Helaine and Jery Schwartz. *Official Price Guide Holiday Collectibles*.New York, NY: House of Collectibles, 1991.

Hart, Cynthia and John Grossman and Priscilla Dunhill. *Victorian Scrapbook*. New York, NY: Workman Publishing, 1989.

Hetchtlinger, Adelaide and Wilbur Cross. *The Complete Book of Paper Collectibles*. New York: Coward, McCann and Georghegan, Ind., 1972.

Holder, Judith. *Sweethearts and Valentines*. New York, NY: A & W Publishers, Inc., 1980.

Ketchum, Jr., William C. *Holiday Ornaments and Antiques*. New York, NY: Alfred A. Knopf, 1990.

Kirsch, Francine. *Chromos: A Guide to Paper Collectibles*. San Diego: A. S. Barnes & Co., 1981

Kreider, Katherine. *Valentines*. Atglen, PA: Schiffer Publishing, 1996.

Lasansky, Jeanette. *Holiday Paper Honeycomb*. Lewisburg, PA: Oral Traditions Project, 1993.

Lee, Ruth Web. *A History of Valentines*. New York: Studio Productions, Inc., 1952.

Nicholson, Susan Brown. *The Encyclopedia of Antique Postcards*. Radnor, Pa: WallaceHomestead Book Co., 1994.

Pieske, Christa. *Das ABC des Luxuspapiers*. Berlin, Germany: Staatliche Museen Preubischer, 1983.

Pulati, Evalene. *Illustrated Valentine Primer with Rarity and Values*. Santa Ana, CA: Evalene Pulati, 1995.

Pulati, Evalene. *National Valentine Collectors Newsletter*. Santa Ana, CA: National Valentine Collectors Association, Summer, 1977-Spring,1996.

Reed, Robert. *Paper Collectibles: The Essential Buyer's Guide*. Radnor, PA: Wallace-Homestead Co., 1995.

Staff, Frank. *The Valentine and its Origins*. New York: Frederick A. Praeger, 1969.

Stern, Michael and David Longest. *The Collector's Encyclopedia of Disneyana,* Paducah, KY: Collectors Books, 1996.

Glossary

Air brushed: fine spray of paint applied through means of a hollow brush into which paint was deposited. Process gave cards a soft shaded effect.

Booklet: small, cardboard covered book with sentimental message illustrated by chromolithographs.

Chromolithography: process by which each separate color required individual steel dies subsequently printed one upon another up to 26 plates.

Comic valentines: category of cards which often ridiculed or poked fun, in varying degrees of subtlety and good taste, at the concept of romantic love.

Embossed: process by which chromolithographs were pressed by patterned pressing dies to give a three-dimensional effect.

Fold-down: card with large back and smaller sized front which folds out (through pull-like hinges) to reveal three-dimensional scene.

Fold-out: card with equally sized sides which folds out (through pull-like hinges) to reveal three-dimensional scene.

Four color printing: process which reduced all colors to black, yellow, blue, and red. All colors were subsequently printed from these four colors.

French fold: one sheet of paper folded in half twice as form of greeting card.

Glans bilder: German term for embossed chromolithographs with a high sheen.

Honeycomb: sheets of colored tissue, glued, and folded flat which when opened appear as the cells of a bee's honeycomb.

Ladder: narrow strip of paper which connects chromolithographs after embossing die removed any unwanted paper.

Mechanical (early): Pre-1880s card which "moves" through means of a pull tab to reveal a second design.

Mechanical (later): Post-1890s animated card which "moves" through means of pull tabs, rivets, and folding paper.

Novelty: fans, hanging valentines, wall pickets, and other utilitarian cards. Termed such because they deviated from the traditional style cards.

Photo print: process by which a photographic image is printed on valentine in tones of black, gray, and white.

Swags: complete, uncut sheets of chromolithographed pictures attached by means of narrow strips of paper referred to as ladders.

Index